Beaufort
Special

Bruce Robertson

LONDON

IAN ALLAN LTD

Contents

Beaufort special corrs 5712 – TH

First published 1976
Second impression 1990

ISBN 0 7110 0667 9

Published by Ian Allan Ltd, Shepperton, Surrey,
and printed by in the United Kingdom by Ian Allan
Printing Ltd at its works at Coombelands in
Runnymede, England.

Introduction

Designed as a torpedo-bomber and used more often as an ordinary bomber, the Beaufort flew more hours on training than on operations, lost more of its numbers by accident than by enemy action, and did more operational sorties in a close support role than on anti-shipping work. Its attacks on enemy warships were in general disappointing, but the type did have some notable successes against merchant ships.

Used in the United Kingdom in the early war years, there followed a time, in mid-1942, when the Beaufort was operational only in the Middle East—and after 1943 it was operational only in the Far East. This meant that the sphere of Beaufort operations shifted eastward as the war progressed.

Some who flew Beauforts regularly, swore by them; many who flew them occasionally, swore about them! This Beaufort Special aims to tell the overall story of this controversial aircraft and highlight many of the incidents in its career.

I wish to thank all those who have assisted in my researches and record my appreciation of the willing help I have always received from R. C. B. Ashworth, Chaz Bowyer, M. J. F. Bowyer, J. D. Brown, Peter G. Cooksley for drawings and map work, J. J. Halley, J. D. Oughton, Alfred Price, Eric Taylor and William Webster.

Organisations that have given particular assistance are the Australian War Memorial, British Aircraft Corporation, Public Archives of Canada, Imperial War Museum, Public Record Office (Great Britain) and the South African Air Force.

London 1975   *Bruce Robertson*

Not Fully Jigged~ The First Five

When Britain went to war in September, 1939, the bombers in front-line service were twin-engined Wellingtons, Whitleys and Blenheims; all modern monoplanes with retractable undercarriages and completely enclosed cockpits. The fighters were the sleek Hurricane, and the Spitfire which had just reached squadron service. Yet the standard RAF torpedo-bomber was an antiquated biplane with an open cockpit and fixed undercarriage—the Vickers Vildebeest.

It was not that the torpedo-bombing role had been overlooked, but that its function was complicated and involved technical problems that took time to solve. The Air Ministry had circulated in 1935 Specification M15/35 for a three-seat, land-based twin-engined reconnaissance bomber with internal stowage for a torpedo. Also issued that year was Specification G24/35 for a twin-engined general reconnaissance aircraft. Following representations by the aircraft firms tendering designs, Avro, Blackburn and Bristol, the Air Staff agreed to consider a single aircraft type to meet the two requirements.

The Bristol Aeroplane Company's submission of their Type 150 three-seat torpedo-bomber was, after consultation with the Air Ministry, changed to a four-seat torpedo-bomber with general reconnaissance capability designated Type 152. (The intervening Type 151 was a design to a completely different requirement for a high-speed fighter.)

Bristol faced strong competition. Avro were anxious to meet the general reconnaissance requirement. The term 'general' is rather misleading, it meant in effect 'maritime'. The new aircraft was intended to replace the Anson that Avro had in production for the task. They lost the contract, but their Anson remained in production for years—as a trainer; while the reconnaissance role was met by purchasing Lockheed Hudsons from America.

Blackburn too, was a strong contender with their B26 design; moreover they had years of experience of building torpedo-bombers for the Fleet Air Arm and foreign governments. Nevertheless, the Bristol Aeroplane Company were awarded a contract on August 22, 1936, for the delivery of 78 aircraft to a production standard given in Air Staff Specification 10/36. The usual qualifying clause on the satisfactory completion of trials by a prototype was waived. The Air Staff had taken the unprecedented step of ordering straight from the drawing board. This was partly due to the urgent need for a Vildebeest replacement, the RAF expansion programme, and the proven basis of the new aircraft.

Bristol had based their design on the Blenheim (Bristol Type 142) then undergoing prototype trials. It had the same basic planform, but was slightly larger—a matter of 18 inches in span. The nose had been brought forward and the turret moved slightly back to maintain the centre of gravity, and the fuselage enlarged to include a new crew station. Since a normal bomb-bay for selective dropping

was required for the maritime role, the torpedo could not be carried entirely enclosed, but the Air Staff had accepted the Bristol proposal for a recessed carriage of this weapon. Because of the increased weight, apart from carrying a torpedo, the 880hp Perseus engine was planned in place of the 840hp Mercury engines of the Blenheim.

Altogether 320 Beauforts were initially required. Bristol had been given the limited order of 78 because the Blenheim's success meant that Bristol's own capacity at Filton was limited. The Company were building Hawker Audax biplanes as trainers and the Blenheim had attracted foreign orders as well as large-scale RAF orders. Moreover, the Blenheims and Beauforts were much larger aircraft than the existing erecting sheds had been designed for when they had been built in 1916. The work force had risen from 4 000 to over 8 000 in the mid-thirties, but new plant was a requirement that would take time. It was therefore proposed that Blackburn should build the balance of 242.

But the picture suddenly changed. The Air Staff considered the 880hp Perseus engines would be inadequate to give the desired performance and the firm's new 1 130hp Taurus engine was substituted. This engine, while showing promise, had not passed its proving tests and with large-scale Mercury and Perseus production underway, and large-scale Hercules production planned, early Taurus production could not be promised. As a result the plan for Blackburn to build Beauforts was scrapped and they received an order for their B26 design, which went into production with Perseus engines as the Botha—and failed in its intended role.

With production space and engine production delays setting back Beaufort production, work went ahead to

complete the first of the order for prototype testing to iron out any shortcomings. It was at the time of the Munich crisis when the first was completed, but there were delays even before it flew. On the initial ground running tests, the engines overheated and the streamlined engined nacelles designed by Roy Fedden had to be replaced by a conventional gilled ring. The first flight was eventually made on October 15, 1938, and soon after the Air Staff adopted the suggestion of the name Beaufort as being alliterative with Bristol and in keeping with Blenheim.

After some delays through engine trouble, the first Beaufort (L4441) was sent to the Aeroplane and Armament Experimental Establishment at Martlesham Heath for type trials on April 17, 1939. While there, engine cowling problems persisted and the aircraft was returned to Filton for further attention five weeks later. Meanwhile, to facilitate output, the Air Ministry agreed to accept the next four aircraft, like the first, 'not fully-jigged'. This was no idle phrase. It virtually branded the first five as prototypes.

A condition of aircraft contracts was that parts should be interchangeable. Aircraft assembled without the approved jigs, giving precise positions for locating drilling and riveting, meant that standard spares might not be usable. Such aircraft were normally marked 'Not to be sent overseas' in the cockpit and 'Repair by makers only' stencilled on all bulkheads. It also meant that service maintenance and modification leaflets had in this case to bear the qualifying words 'Not applicable to aircraft L4441 to L4445 inclusive'.

Jigging was of particular importance to the Beaufort, for it was designed to be built compartmented to permit dispersed production, a factor that was to lead to its

Top: The prototype Beaufort as it first appeared in 1938 with original engine nacelles designed by Roy Fedden. The apron-type undercarriage covers caused the aircraft to yaw on landing if the wheels did not drop evenly because of the uneven drag these imposed. / *Bristol Aeroplane Company*

Above left: The prototype Beaufort shapes up to production form with gilled engine cooling and undercarriage modified. At the left is a Blackburn Skua used as a test-bed at Filton and to the right Hart and Audax trainers and beyond a Tiger Moth of No 2 Elementary Reserve Flying Training School at Filton, where experimental and production operation aircraft on test flights had to take their turn with pupils doing circuits and bumps. / *Bristol Aeroplane Company*

Above: The second Beaufort, delivered in 1939, had the standard bomber camouflage of the period, uppersurfaces in a disruptive pattern of dark green and dark earth (the official description for the shade of brown) and undersurface matt black. It differs from the prototype by bomb aiming panels in the nose but only in the first nine aircraft were the panels curved. / *Bristol Aeroplane Company*

production in railway workshops the other side of the world.

Because of the negotiations then pending with the Australians, interested in licence production, the Beaufort was presented in glowing terms by the Air Ministry and they were a little sensitive about criticism. The foreign press had not shared their enthusiasm. They called the Beaufort a version of the Blenheim and pointed out that with the increased accommodation it would undoubtedly be slower. The Air Ministry then issued a statement to, as they put it, dispel erroneous impressions. The machine is of an entirely new design, they stated, and despite its improved accommodation and slightly larger dimensions, it probably ranks as the world's fastest bomber.

Brave words. The Beaufort, with an engine as yet unproven, had much to live up to.

Mainly for Mining ~ The Beaufort Goes Operational

By the declaration of war on September 3, 1939, a firm programme had been made for using the first few Beauforts in the interests of the many to come. L4441, the first, was to continue at Filton on engine endurance tests. L4442 nearing completion was to be used for armament trials, L4443 was to be kept at Filton to assist with engine cooling trials, while L4444, fitted with dual controls, would go to the Central Flying School for handling and pilots' notes to be prepared. The fifth (L4445) was earmarked for the Torpedo Development Unit, while the 6th to 9th Beauforts (L4446-4449) were to be used for intensive flying trials by No 22 Squadron at Thorney Island. This intensive use, a normal procedure, was to force out snags that could arise in service, to give a chance for preventative modifications to be incorporated on those yet to leave the production lines. Meanwhile, the total on order had been increased to 350.

L4446, the first true, fully-jigged, Beaufort was sent to No 22 Squadron at Thorney Island on November 24, 1939; it had been preceded nine days earlier by L4447. Neither were to survive the working-up period for the Beaufort was found to have a marked tendency to swing on take-off and landing. As L4447 set out on a practice flight, with a pilot completely new to the type on January 8, 1940, it swung, hit a boundary hedge and was completely wrecked. The crew survived but the salvage, returned to Filton, was valued merely by the weight of metal.

Eight days later L4446 crashed into the sea 50 yards off Fort Blockhouse, Portsmouth. The crew were rescued and the accident was put down to mishandling by a pilot unfamiliar with the type. A third accident that January came on the 20th. Another victim of the vicious swing on take-off, L4458 headed towards a clump of trees bounding the airfield. The pilot applied the brakes causing a side-skid on the wheels that broke the undercarriage and the Beaufort dropped on to its belly.

Trials continued with other production deliveries, all going to No 22 Squadron except L4456 for type trials and L4448 which had arrived in Australia. By the same token some eighty Australians had come to Bristol to learn how to build Beauforts, but that is another story related later.

So far, little had been done beyond familiarising the crews of No 22 Squadron with flying the Beaufort. It was not only in aircraft deliveries that Coastal Command were behind Bomber and Fighter Commands, but also in arranging operational training. This was because unlike the other two Commands, in the so-called Phoney War period, Coastal Command had been actively engaged on operations since the first day of the war.

Most crews at this time had received some specialist training at the pre-war School of General Reconnaissance at Thorney Island or the Torpedo Training School, Gosport. To train new crews for replacements and expansion, a Coastal Command landplane pilots' pool was formed at Silloth in November 1939 to instruct on operational aircraft, and give advance training to wireless operators and air gunners. While Ansons and Hudsons were available for this training, Beauforts were not. In March 1940 the unit was renamed the Coastal Command Operational Training Unit, by which time the first Beauforts were being delivered to the unit.

But for No 22, the first Beaufort squadron, much more training was needed, particularly in torpedo dropping. The torpedo had to be dropped in a straight and level low approach run. Dropping in a dive would cause 'porpoising' in the torpedo running, when it would be apt to go completely beneath a ship without hitting, or hit well above the waterline. Even to line up with a ship meant practice in low level flying, and training in ship speed estimation, let alone ship recognition training. Co-operation with naval ships for simulated attacks was essential.

But torpedo-bombing was not at the time the Beauforts' major role. The magnetic mine was to play an important part in the war. The Navy had ordered the mine in quantity in 1939 and wisely the Navy decided not to unleash the weapon until there were sufficient numbers to be used effectively. The Germans were already using a similar weapon and the Chiefs of Staff jointly agreed that Coastal Command, and Bomber Command as required, would deliver the British equivalent to areas designated by the Navy. The code-word 'Gardening' was given to this

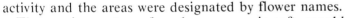

Above: No 22 Squadron became operational at North Coates in 1940. Beaufort L4449 seen in the foreground bore a charmed life. It was delivered to the squadron on November 24, 1939, went on to serve in Nos 217 and 86 Squadrons, No 5 OTU and No 2 Torpedo Training Unit before being discarded June 19, 1945. / *IWM*

Below: The fifth production Beaufort L4445 was used by the Torpedo Development Unit from October 27, 1937, for armament trials and commenced torpedo dropping trials from May 1940, and is seen here with a biplane torpedo-bomber Swordfish in the background. After trials it was used by No 5 OTU where, on March 1, 1942, a trainee pilot misjudged height flying it over the water. A propeller hit the surface and broke up. The Beaufort, unable to maintain height on one engine, stalled and crashed.

Left: Beauforts of No 22 Squadron at North Coates, June 1940. / *IWM*

Bottom: Beaufort of No 22 Squadron seen after sweeping low over a German motor ship of a convoy off the Dutch coast. / *IWM*

activity and the areas were designated by flower names.

The requirement was for a long-range aircraft, capable of accurate navigation, to approach German estuaries, harbour approaches and sea lanes unobtrusively at night, at a speed not exceeding 200mph, and drop a mine from 500 feet accurately into 30 feet or more of water. A Mk 1 mine of 1 500lb had been designed to be carried by torpedo-carrying aircraft, so that the allocation of Beauforts for this task was inevitable. Since the dropping required was on a scale beyond the capacity of the only Beaufort squadron, Bomber Command's Hampden squadrons were also diverted to this task. Beauforts and Hampdens both engaged in tests to discover from how far on a moonlight night the splash of a dropping mine could be seen by coast watchers.

Due to the Beaufort's more limited range, Coastal Command were made responsible for mining the Ems and Jade-Weser estuaries and Bomber Command all other areas. The mining was to have started during the moonlight period April 18 to 25, and No 22 Squadron moved from Thorney Island to North Coates, near Grimsby on the Lincolnshire coast, on April 9 in preparation. That very day the Germans invaded Denmark and Norway—the 'Phoney War' was over. As a result, the mining programme was brought forward. On the night of April 15/16, 1940, nine Beauforts of No 22 Squadron each carrying a mine, led by Wg Cdr H. V. Mellor, took off at intervals to lay mines in Schilling Roads, just north of Wilhelmshaven; of these L4465 failed to return. The Beaufort was operational.

Beaufort Bombers. Early Operations, 1940

The Beaufort may be classed generally as a torpedo-bomber and planned for regular mining missions, but by far the majority of its missions were with conventional bombs. The normal bomb load was four 250lb bombs or two 500lb bombs mainly of three types, semi-armour piercing (SAP) for attacking shipping, anti-submarine (AS) with depth exploders or general purpose (GP) for warehouse attacks. Maximum bomb load was 2 000lb and with a special carrier a 2 000lb bomb could be carried. It was a Beaufort that dropped the first British 2 000lb bomb, on May 7, 1940, aimed at a German cruiser anchored off Norderney.

The bomb bay of the Beaufort could be fitted with various combinations of carriers. They were lowered mechanically onto the bombs and raised by a geared bomb hoist which was an integral fitting of the aircraft. There was also provision for a Universal No 1 bomb carrier to be fitted under the wings. This would permit the carriage of bombs additional to the bombs stowed internally in short-range operations such as bombing an enemy submarine sighted off-shore.

The Beaufort was, unsuitable as a high level bomber. Tests of L4456 on bombing ranges, flying from Boscombe Down, were disappointing. When bombs were released at 10 000ft at a true air speed of 238mph, the aircraft proved, in the words of the test pilot—'An exceptionally poor bombing platform, being subject to an excessive and continuous roll which made determination of drift particularly difficult. Bombing was also done at lower speeds than the full cruising speed in the hope of finding more stable conditions, but without success'. Fortunately it was reasonably satisfactory at low-level.

Bombing was forced on the Beaufort by events. The massive German attack on France and the Low Countries, in May, following on the invasion of Norway and Denmark, brought the possibility of invasion of the British Isles and desperate measures were needed. Beauforts were sent out to bomb Waalhaven on the night of May 12/13 and on May 18/19 with Hudsons they vied with Bomber Command by attacking oil refineries at Bremen and Hamburg. Five Beauforts, each carrying four 250lb GP bombs, attacked oil tanks at Rotterdam on May 20/21. Then a daylight raid was suddenly ordered on May 25 when German E-boats were reported at Ymuiden.

Unfortunately the Beaufort was still plagued with engine troubles. That spring L4468 on test at Filton crashed into the Severn, then L4443 crashed on experimental work. The commander of No 22 Squadron, Wg Cdr R. E. X. Mack, DFC, was lost at sea in May on a mining sortie through an engine failure on L4450.

There was a tragic end to a sortie on June 6 bombing oil dumps at Ghent. When L9797 was returning to North Coates, the airfield lighting could not be put on because an enemy aircraft was in the district. The Beaufort was diverted northwards along the coast. On the way

searchlights probed the sky and dazzled the pilot who momentarily dived. This caused terrific vibration and fumes came up from the rear, presumably the combined result of anti-aircraft sustained damage over Belgium and the dive. The pilot, believing the aircraft was shaking to pieces, ordered the crew to bale out, set the controls to take the abandoned aircraft out to sea, and left by parachute. He and the observer landed safely, but unbeknown to them the wireless operator and air gunner did not bale out and it is possible that they were overcome by fumes. They remained in the Beaufort which turned and dived into a row of cottages at Ashington in Cumberland, killing the two RAF men and injuring four civilians.

Not only because their engines were unreliable, but also because the crews were not yet trained in torpedo-dropping, the Beauforts were denied an early strike at the German battlecruiser *Scharnhorst* which was to plague them for the next two years. A Blenheim crew had sighted her on June 10, returning from the foray in which she had sunk the aircraft carrier HMS *Glorious* two days previously. When a strike was planned by Skuas operating from HMS *Ark Royal* three nights later, the Beauforts of No 22 Squadron merely played a diversionary role by attacking Vaernes airfield near Trondheim to prevent German fighters taking off and interfering with the Skuas. After the attack the *Scharnhorst* did one of her disappearing acts.

There was now a second Beaufort squadron, No 42. Their first Beauforts, received in April, gradually replaced

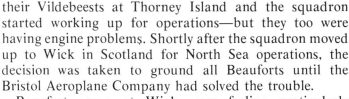

their Vildebeests at Thorney Island and the squadron started working up for operations—but they too were having engine problems. Shortly after the squadron moved up to Wick in Scotland for North Sea operations, the decision was taken to ground all Beauforts until the Bristol Aeroplane Company had solved the trouble.

Beaufort crews at Wick were feeling particularly frustrated when it was reported that the *Scharnhorst* had been re-sighted. HM Submarine *Clyde* fired torpedoes at her at 02.35 hrs on June 21 eight miles off the Norwegian coast; causing her to reduce speed. The station intelligence officer at Wick kept the crews briefed and they, realising the chance that was being missed, pressed their Commanding Officer to get the ban on flying lifted. Wg Cdr H. Waring went to see the station commander, and was putting his case when the Group Captain was called to the telephone by the Commander-in-Chief, Coastal Command, Air Chief Marshal F. W. Bowhill. In the course of conversation the station commander mentioned Wg Cdr Waring's request that the squadron should be allowed to attack in spite of the uncertainty of their engines. The ban was lifted and nine Beauforts set out.

The Germans gave No 42 Squadron credit for a higher standard of training than they had attained, for as the Beauforts approached Trondheim the destroyers attendant on the *Scharnhorst* manoeuvred as if expecting a torpedo-attack, whereas the Beauforts delivered a dive-bombing attack with 500lb armour piercing bombs. As the attack was made close to the Norwegian shore, some

Top: Originally earmarked for test as a civil transport version, a project dropped after war was declared, L4456 was completed to normal Beaufort standard and went to Boscombe Down for trials fitted with Taurus II engines. It was damaged by enemy action during the Battle of Britain; subsequently repaired, it was flown at No 5 OTU, Turnberry where it crashed in November 1942. Repaired again, it was finally wrecked in June 1943 when serving No 51 OTU. / *Bristol Aeroplane Company*

Above left: Beauforts of the second squadron to be equipped with the type, No 42. Aircraft 'S' in the foreground flew 300 hours with the squadron from December 1940 until it went missing April 9, 1942.

Above: Black Beaufort. One of the first Beauforts to serve with No 217 Squadron, used for night raids on the occupied French west coast ports from St Eval, has matt black anti-searchlight undersurfaces in place of the usual sky shade. / *IWM*

50 Messerschmitt Bf109s swarmed over to chase the Beauforts back, shooting three down. But apart from these losses, there were no others. The engines gave no trouble on this occasion.

No 48 Squadron had been receiving Beauforts from May 1940, but these were withdrawn and transferred to No 217 Squadron before the squadron became operational with the type. No 217 Squadron received their first Beauforts in September and after taking over No 48's Beauforts in November at St Eval, were ready for operations.

Beauforts at Bristol, Production, Modification and Designation 1940

At this time there was no alternative to the Beaufort as a long distance strike aircraft and unlike the Blenheim which was produced by the parent firm and under contract by Avros and in a shadow factory operated by Rootes, Beaufort production centred entirely on Bristol. The importance of Bristol in the war was its docks and associated food and oil installations, together with its aircraft, aero engine and aircraft component factories. Of the aircraft industry, the most important single unit was the large factory at Filton, with its adjacent aero engine works and the separate Rodney Works specialising in general pressings, cowlings and exhausts. In mid-1939, this complex was the largest single aircraft manufacturing area in the world.

The first of the Luftwaffe's attacks on this complex in 1940 was a chance affair. Bristol was the night target on June 24 and the works were not located. A single bomber on July 4 dropped two bombs by a barrage balloon winch and was probably lost, the crew unaware that they were flying through a balloon barrage.

The first direct attack, in the early evening of August 14, was by three Ju88s which were part of far-ranging Luftwaffe attacks the length and breadth of England. These attacks were driven off by anti-aircraft guns, but in the night raids that followed on Bristol and its environs it was inevitable that some bombs would fall withing the 2½ million square feet of aircraft factory roofage.

At this time, while the Battle of Britain was at its height, it was decided that Beauforts in service would be flown into Filton for the Taurus engines to be modified. By the end of August 1940, 254 Beauforts had been delivered of which 134 were in maintenance units awaiting engines or engine modifications. Those in service at this time were distributed as follows:—

No 22 Squadron	25
No 42 Squadron	23
No 48 Squadron	19
No 217 Squadron	14
No 1 Operational Training Unit	18
Torpedo Training Unit	13
Torpedo Development Unit	1
Central Flying School	2
On experimental work	5
Total in service (1.9.40)	120

Both the Beaufort and its engine designations, have caused some confusion over the years. The Taurus engine in its Mk III form had been standard for the Beaufort, but the Mk II Taurus was found to be more satisfactory and was fitted when possible. In September 1939 the Air Ministry had issued notification that 'The name of the Bristol general reconnaissance and torpedo-bomber when fitted with two Taurus Mk III engines is Beaufort I and when fitted with two Taurus Mk II engines is Beaufort II'.

So it was as Beauforts Mks I and II that the aircraft were flown in to Filton for modification and as Mk IIs they departed, since Bristol standardised on a Taurus II. But this was a modified Taurus II, provisionally called the IIA, but when the modifications were incorporated on production, the engine became the Taurus VI.

Since all Beauforts were themselves all now designated Mk II, it was decided to cancel the original notification and from the end of the year all Beauforts having either IIA or VI engines became Mk I. Re-engined later with more powerful Taurus XII or XVI engines, the Mk I designation still stood. Mk II was later allotted to aircraft fitted with the Pratt & Whitney Twin Wasp engines, also the standard power unit of the Australian-built versions. To tabulate the Beaufort versions and their designations:

Mk	Engines	Period
I	2 x Bristol Taurus III	1939-40
I	2 x Bristol Taurus II/IIA/VI	1940-44
I	2 x Bristol Taurus XII/XVI	1941-45
II*	2 x Bristol Taurus II	1939-40
II	2 x P & W Twin Wasp S3C4G	1941-46
III	2 x Rolls-Royce Merlin XX	Project only
IV	2 x Bristol Taurus XX	Experiment only

Designation cancelled, 1940

Before the engine modification programme was complete at Filton, stark tragedy came to the plant shortly before midday on September 25, when a formation of German bombers unloaded directly over the main factory area. Over 100 bombs fell within the 732 acres owned by the Company. While most of the bombs fell on the airfield or between buildings, doing relatively little damage, two shelters received direct hits. Nearly a hundred workers died and well over that number were injured.

Bristol's ordeal continued as the Germans turned to their nightly blitz. On the night of November 24/25 the bombing was very widespread, but two key aircraft component plants were hit and public utility services, particularly water supply, were affected; 171 were killed in the city area and a rather larger number injured, inevitably including a number of Bristol workers. An estimated force of 100 enemy bombers followed up the attack on the night of December 2/3 before the city had carried out its full repairs. The Bristol factories were not hit, but were indirectly affected by hits on electricity feeders and hits on the railways including each of the three stations. Four nights later came a lighter attack, but there were hits again on component factories and over 152 casualties were inflicted.

These were the conditions under which the Beaufort builders lived in late 1940. They were working in a key target area and living under frequent attack, first by day

Right: King George VI and Queen Elizabeth, now the Queen Mother, pay a wartime visit to the Bristol Aeroplane Company at Filton and are seen after viewing an early production Beaufort. The curved perspex nose panels tended to give distorted vision and were replaced. / *IWM*

and then by night. Apart from the likelihood of violent death or injury, there were hundreds of Bristol employees bombed out of their homes and those with shattered roofs and windows in their homes were relatively lucky. For many days in late 1940 there was no water, gas or electricity in the city area. Soup kitchens were brought into the factory and emergency generators used to keep essential services going.

Yet production still went on. By the end of the year 400 Beauforts had been delivered and further orders had been placed. Modifications were going on all the time and L9863 was at this time being flown on cabin heating trials and propeller de-icing tests. A major change proposed, the substituting of Pratt & Whitney Twin Wasp engines, had been mooted as early as April 1940, but had been held in abeyance as it was hoped that the modified Taurus engines would give the reliability so essential to a maritime aircraft.

Above: The Bristol Taurus, 14-cylinder, twin-row, sleeve-valve, piston-engine that powered the Beaufort gave an output of 1,065hp at 5 000 feet, and could fit into a cowling just under four feet in diameter. This picture shows a Taurus engine being replaced on a Beaufort in November 1940. / IWM

Left: To give protection against attack from under the tail, a blind spot for the crew, a remotely fired .303 Browning machine-gun mounted in a special chin turret, similar to the Blenheim IVF, was introduced in 1940. It was fed from the prone bombing position, and expended rounds were ejected through the chute at the bottom of the cover. The installation did not prove effective and some units had them removed. / IWM

Right: A No 22 Squadron modification to give added protection—a .303 VGO machine-gun mounted in the entry hatch with a guide to prevent the wing being hit. / IWM

Torpedoes and Tonnage. Defensive to Offensive 1940~41

The Beaufort grounding was cancelled in August 1940 as modified aircraft returned to their units. With three squadrons now equipped with Beauforts, No 22 in the east, No 42 at the north of Scotland using both Leuchars and Wick and No 217 on the South-West peninsula, Coastal Command had a potential torpedo-strike force. Torpedo-dropping training was put in hand while the Battle of Britain was still at its height.

While air battles raged over South-East England, Beauforts of No 22 Squadron on September 11 made the first RAF torpedo attack of the war. Five took off from North Coates and though failing to meet the escort fighters over Detling, set off to attack a convoy of three merchant vessels off Ostend. Three torpedoes failed to drop, one burst prematurely, but one hit a 6,000-ton ship.

Before the month was out the squadron had carried out seven more torpedo attacks, at a time when it was thought any German merchant ship might well be part of a convoy forming up for the invasion of Britain.

Until the end of 1940, No 22 Squadron made 36 torpedo attacks in the Channel area and No 42 Squadron mounted two attacks from Scotland. It was estimated that in this period Beauforts attacked 55 vessels, hitting ten totalling 51 000 tons. The hit rate was 18.5 per cent of torpedoes dropped, average dropping height was 68 feet—below mast level in some cases—and average range of release was 670 yards from the target.

Torpedo attack practices also had their dangers. The pilot of L9942 of No 42 Squadron misjudged his height on September 30, 1940. One airscrew bent when it tipped the water and this caused loss of power. The aircraft forced landed in the sea and sank to the bottom of Sinclair's Bay, Caithness; the crew escaped without injury.

Normal bombing attacks and 'Rover patrols' with bombs continued. Once during October the Beauforts of No 22 Squadron were briefed to attack the German passenger liners *Bremen* and *Europa* at Bremerhaven. At times, detachments were sent to St Eval for attacks on ports along the enemy-occupied western seaboard of France. After a night bombing raid on Bordeaux on December 18, L9823 force-landed in the sea three miles south of the Needles, and sank in four minutes. The crew could not release the dinghy but three members were picked up by a Free-French patrol vessel.

The German cruiser *Hipper*, having sustained damage in action with HMS *Berwick* and HMS *Bonaventure*, went into dry dock at Brest on January 2, 1941, for precisely a month. Beauforts were among the Coastal Command aircraft bombing the dock area, but from January 17 to 31 weather precluded attacks. The cruiser left on February 3 but was back twelve days later, the day three Beauforts were despatched to sink her. None returned.

In the same way that Fighter Command, having recovered from losses in the Battle of Britain, was taking the offensive by sweeps over occupied France, so Coastal Command were sending out Beauforts on offensive patrols in the spring of 1941. At 13.33hrs on April 1 three Beauforts on a roving strike against shipping off the Danish coast sighted five merchant vessels, each of some 2 000 tons, off Horns Reef. One ship straggling behind the others was selected as the victim and as the Beauforts left the area it was enveloped in black smoke.

Perhaps it was coincidence that made the Luftwaffe resume night operations on a fairly substantial scale, with Bristol their target on the night of April 3/4. The heat-treatment plant of the factory was damaged on this occasion. The following night No 217's base at St Eval was attacked by two enemy aircraft which damaged Hurricanes with their machine-gun fire, but no Beauforts were affected.

The German battle cruisers *Scharnhorst* and *Gneisenau,* after being active against British trade routes in the Atlantic, made Brest, on the west coast of France, their base for further forays. Constituting a danger to our life-line to America, the elimination of the ships was a strategic priority and both Bomber and Coastal Command pounded their berths at Brest from late March 1941 once it was established by photographic reconnaissance precisely where they were. After a series of attacks by aircraft of Bomber Command an unexploded bomb in the dry dock caused the Germans to move the *Gneisenau* alongside a quay in the inner harbour, Rade Abri. This move was revealed within hours by a Spitfire on one of the regular photographic reconnaissance sorties that kept the German ships under surveillance.

Attacks were intensified; on the night of April 4/5 39 Wellingtons, 11 Hampdens and 4 Manchesters bombed Brest, spreading action over 2½ hours. The ships were clearly seen, one in dry dock and one alongside the quay of the torpedo station. The following morning ten Hampdens set out to make use of cloud cover for the approach, for it would be suicidal to attack in clear daylight. As the weather cleared *en route*, the Hampdens had to abandon their attack and return, except for one that fell into the sea off Ushant.

To be closer at hand in case the German ships were to break out into the Atlantic, No 22 Squadron at North Coates had already been alerted to send a detachment of Beauforts to St Eval in Cornwall. This area was No 217 Squadron's sphere, but No 22 had the experience. Now that the *Gneisenau* was floating, a torpedo attack could well sink her and the Beauforts were ordered to make the attempt.

It was a most dangerous mission. There was the possibility of fighter interception before reaching the port, then there were three flak ships in the harbour, a mole bristling with anti-aircraft guns, and various shore batteries apart from the anti-aircraft defences of the ships in harbour. The run-in would have to be low over the mole, the torpedo dropped close to the target, the exit a steep banked turn to avoid rising ground beyond.

Six Beauforts were ordered to strike in the early morning of April 6, but only three took off together—the others being bogged down under the weight of their torpedoes. After strenuous efforts one other Beaufort

Above: Torpedo training. The torpedo was recessed into the bomb bay and a cable on a tensioned drum, and an air tail, ensured a straight and level drop. Although a Beaufort might well dive before attacking, satisfactory torpedo release could only be made in level flight. / *via Chaz Bowyer*

Right: Flying Officer Kenneth Campbell, posthumously awarded the Victoria Cross for his gallant attempt to torpedo the *Gneisenau* at Brest, April 6, 1941, flying No 22 Squadron Beaufort N1016 coded OA.X./ *via IWM*

did get away, but only one of those taking off found the target.

The pilot of Beaufort N1016 located the target and made a run-in over flak ships at barely mast height, launching the torpedo at 500 yards range. Running true, the torpedo smacked into the side of the *Gneisenau* damaging her below the waterline and necessitating repairs before any break-out was possible. This Beaufort did not return but for his determination the pilot, Flying Officer K. Campbell, was awarded the Victoria Cross posthumously and his observer, Sgt J. P. Scott, received the Distinguished Flying Medal; the other crew members were Sgts R. W. Hillman and W. Mallis.

That same day three Beauforts of No 217 Squadron attacked enemy destroyers off Morlaix and were attacked in turn by Bf109s. One Beaufort was lost and another wrecked on landing. No 217 Squadron was now intensively engaged in anti-shipping work in the south-west. On April 9, when a Spitfire of the PRU brought photos of a large merchant vessel escorted by naval units off Ushant, three Beauforts set out and hit a merchant ship of 3 000 tons north of the Ile de Bas. This was considered undersize for the period to warrant torpedoes which were in short supply. Ships of 6 000 tons plus were considered worth torpedo expenditure, but in this case its naval escort pointed to a particularly valuable cargo. But once on patrol with torpedo, it was difficult not to use it on the first enemy ship presented. A Beaufort crew on a night mission spotted five vessels of some 1 000 tons forty miles off Lodbierg and attacked.

Yet another attack on Bristol on the night of April 11/12 resulted in over a hundred citizens being killed and, apart from affecting many workers, there were hits on parts of the works, including the central wages department and the Winterstoke Road plant. Two nights later St Eval was again attacked. One stick of bombs fell just outside the perimeter, just too far away to damage dispersed Beauforts and a second stick fell on the married quarters, which were then unoccupied.

Meanwhile, while Bomber Command continued to pound Brest with the hope of damaging the ships to prevent them moving out, No 217 Squadron Beauforts went on a mining programme off Brest in case they did break out. One pilot, on the night of April 15/16, reported that his mine exploded on contact with the water. In the early hours of the same morning a Beaufort was sent after much smaller fry, merchant ships on the Orne at Caen. Unable to locate them, the Beaufort deposited its bombs on the local marshalling yards.

The next night, in contrast to Bomber Command's 100-plus aircraft raids on Brest, Coastal Command started a series of mini-raids with two to six Beauforts and a similar number of Blenheims, aiming for the battle cruisers. Apart from raids, regular patrols were being made by Beauforts, often without incident, but there were occasional surprises. Patrolling along the west coast of France on April 18, the crew of a Beaufort came upon a Heinkel He115. Warning the gunner and making towards it, they saw it jettison its bombs and dive away.

That night, while four Beauforts carried out the routine mining off Brest, another two tried some more intimate mining. One mine was dropped in the harbour area itself; the other was intended to be placed there, but was jettisoned hastily when the Beaufort's cabin roof was shot off by anti-aircraft fire.

The Beaufort/Blenheim mini-blitz continued nightly, weather permitting. On the night of April 25/26 two Beauforts made anti-aircraft batteries their target; that night enemy night fighters intervened and one Beaufort was forced to jettison its bomb load to take evasive action.

Occasionally aircraft would not return from operations, for reasons not attributable to enemy action, including the off-shore mining to Brest which was considered a fairly safe operation as it was done in darkness and the anti-aircraft defences were not involved. And not only from operations, there were also heavy losses during operational training. The feeling of crews was summed up by the pilot of W6527 who had force-landed on April 29 while practising on Transmuir Range. He reported that an engine had failed and that he could not maintain height

Above: A brave attempt by a photographic reconnaissance pilot to secure evidence of the position of the German battle cruisers in Brest. Through the dawn mist the *Scharnhorst* can be seen in dry dock, next to which is an empty dock from which the *Gneisenau* was moved to the quayside position indicated by the lower arrow. The markings are the photographic interpreters' own indications on the negative. / *via Sqn Ldr M. Williamson*

Right: Returning with torpedo. Torpedoes were expensive weapons and unlike bombs could not be jettisoned except in an emergency. The wing flaps can be seen lowered for landing. / *IWM*

on one. The commander of No 42 Squadron endorsed the official report of this accident with the words 'Extremely improbable whether any Beaufort will keep height on one engine. Pilots are beginning to lose confidence in the machines. Strongly recommend re-engining with Twin Wasps'.

Development work was under way to re-engine the Beaufort, but it was not a simple matter of taking out one engine and substituting another, but required extensive changes and re-building with the new engines. Meanwhile, the more powerful Taurus XII engines were being fitted to aircraft coming off the lines.

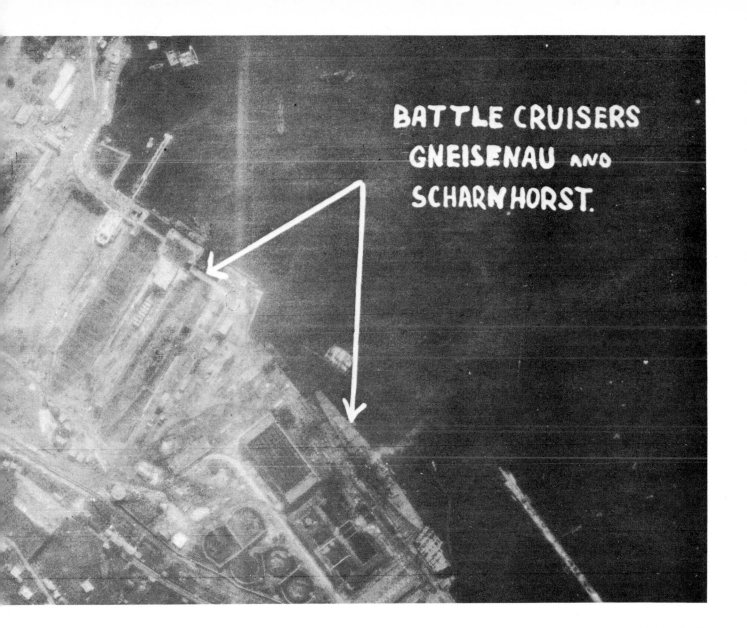

BATTLE CRUISERS
GNEISENAU and
SCHARNHORST.

Peak Strength
UK ~ 1941

Bombing and mining in the Brest area continued and became routine operations, but fraught with danger. W6530 forced to return with a mine, blew up on landing at St Eval on June 10, killing all the crew. Next day, the two Beaufort squadrons covering the North Sea were alerted.

Early on the morning of June 11, 1941 information reached Coastal Command HQ that a German naval force was moving into the Baltic. Presuming it to be making northward along the Norwegian coast, and in the absence of further sighting reports, Beaufort formations, armed with torpedoes were sent out at 23.00 and 23.30hrs next night by No 42 Squadron, from their two bases at Leuchars and Wick, briefed to search a sector of coast from the vicinity of the Lister Light south of Stavanger. At midnight, a Blenheim of No 114 Squadron on standby patrol wirelessed a sighting report of a cruiser and four destroyers, giving position and course. This information, relayed over the air to the Beauforts on search, resulted in three making contact. The capital ship, identified later as the pocket battleship *Lützow*, was closely screened by destroyers as the three Beauforts, 'R', 'W' and 'Y', attacked. In spite of making two runs, 'R's torpedo failed to drop, but the other two were more fortunate and Flt Sgt R. H. Loviett scored a hit. The German ship was severely damaged and limped back towards the Skagerrak.

A few minutes after the attack a bombing force of 11 Blenheims with four more Beauforts left Leuchars to make a follow-up attack, but failed to make contact. The next sighting, by a Blenheim of No 114 Squadron at 06.00hrs, revealed that the ship was crippled and returning to port so that a further torpedo attack, this time by three Beauforts from No 22 Squadron at North Coates, was ordered. These Beauforts left at 09.30hrs but also failed to make contact. This failure was probably due to the limited number searching. Of necessity a small force was employed for in full daylight off South-West Norway the German fighters would be well alerted to the situation. Additionally, the low approach required both for surprise and torpedo attack technique reduced sighting chances further. Three days later the *Lützow* was in dock at Kiel.

At Leuchars No 42 Squadron had good facilities, a pre-war airfield which was probably the best camouflaged in the United Kingdom. Cropped pines were placed around domestic areas to give the appearance of forest and in the camouflage scheme a road appeared to exist cutting across the airfield, including over one hangar. The squadron also tried to improve the Beaufort.

One of the Beaufort's snags was tailwheel shimmy. This wheel often failed to swivel in line with the direction of the aircraft, and because of skidding on landing the tyres were soon worn down. On one occasion a tailwheel became fully jammed at right angles and the tyre had worn down to the canvas by the time the aircraft had come to rest. The Squadron engineer officer designed a controlled castoring

Above: Mission Markings on Beaufort 'W' of No 42 Squadron flown by Flt Sgt R. H. Loviett, showing a Heinkel He115 with which his Beaufort had brushed and the *Lutzow* representation. In general bombing and torpedo attacks were not marked on noses as they were in Bomber Command. In No 42 Squadron the aircraft letter was extended into a name, hence the word 'Wreck'.

Above right: Beaufort of No 42 Squadron on standby at Leuchars carrying a Mk XII torpedo and 42-inch air tail. The control tower personnel at Leuchars complained that the code letters on their aircraft were too inconspicuous, evinced by this photo of L9938 coded AW.Y. / *Royal Canadian Air Force*

Below right: Following the code letter complaint, an airman was directed to make the Leuchars code letters more evident, as seen on AW·K of No 42 Squadron. The individual letter on the nose was made into a name on this squadron.

wheel and had an example made by his fitters for the Bristol works. A few months later Bristol brought out a modification kit to remedy the shimmy.

Fortunately the main undercarriage was very sturdy. It needed to be. The Beaufort might well jettison its bombs, but a torpedo was a different matter and had to be brought back if not used. Such was the strength and rigidity of the undercarriage, the oleos could not be moved with a crowbar when it was held in a maintenance frame, yet in a normal landing, the wheels pumped easily up and down after touch-down by the sheer weight of the aircraft.

Another improvement by No 42 Squadron was the fitting of side guns with shaped plates at the gun ports, to prevent the free-mounted VGOs (Vickers gas-operated guns) from shooting off the wingtips.

A weakness of all Coastal Command aircraft was the lack of an efficient method of keeping the windscreen clear in heavy rain. The Beaufort's shortcomings in this respect were pointedly shown up when Beaufort W6470 crashed on landing at Thorney Island on July 31 through the pilot being blinded by torrential rain. Following the Court of Inquiry, the Air Ministry were pressed to solve the problem but nothing but a partial solution was ever found.

After an intensive year of operations, No 22 Squadron was moved from North Coates back to Thorney Island in June 1941. A Blenheim squadron, No 86, was re-equipped with Beauforts that month and started operational

reconnaissance flights and torpedo-training, and began attacks from North Coates the following November. With four operational squadrons, Coastal Command was at its highest Beaufort strike strength. There were even two more Beaufort squadrons under training. No 489 (New Zealand) Squadron formed at Leuchars on August 12, but due to supply difficulties was re-equipped with Blenheims in January 1942. On August 20, No 415 (Canadian) Squadron formed at Thorney Island and received Beauforts the following month; but this squadron was re-equipped with Hampdens before becoming operational.

From September 1942 some Beauforts were fitted with ASV (Air-to-Surface Vessel) radar to develop techniques of ship detection in the dark or poor visibility. A special Shipping Interceptor Flight of No 217 Squadron was detached to Manston to seek out enemy ships in the Channel, detecting them by radar and dropping flares to illuminate them for attacks by bombs or torpedoes. No 11 Group of Fighter Command were brought in on the project to attack with Hurri-bombers—the bomber version of the Hurricane. A few attacks were carried out, but results were not observed and were not considered successful. For this reason, and the shortage of Beauforts due to overseas requirements, the special flight was withdrawn but the

ASV equipment was retained for squadron use.

Operations continued to take their toll. Some low-level attacks were ordered including a raid on Nantes in October, shipping attacks in November and bombing again in December. No 22 Squadron had by this time been moved again, this time to St Eval specifically for sea mining and bombing attacks in Western France, leaving No 42 Squadron at Leuchars as the only fully trained standby torpedo strike squadron. With the *Tirpitz* at Trondheim to the north, and *Scharnhorst, Gneisenau* and *Prinz Eugen* at Brest to the south, all four Beaufort squadrons had a series of reconnaissance missions and standby periods. All this caused a steady drain on crews and aircraft. At this time No 22 Squadron was warned for service in the Mediterranean; one of their last successes from the UK was the torpedoing and sinking of a large tanker outward bound from Cherbourg.

There was also a steady loss of Beauforts at No 5 (Coastal) Operational Training Unit at Chivenor in North Devon. On the night of August 9 the pilot of L9953 lost control in a squall and his aircraft dived vertically into the River Taw half a mile south-east of the airfield, killing all four crew. Later in the month N1160 with an engine failure, side-slipped out of control into the sea off Saunton

Sands. Three aircrew were also killed in December when W6478, taking off in the dark, suddenly dived into the river bounding the airfield.

But more Beauforts had been ordered, production was well under way, and a new engine was being fitted. And in spite of a move to the East, the Beaufort was to soldier on in the United Kingdom well into 1942.

Beaufort Squadron Code Letters in the United Kingdom

RAF Squadrons

No 22 OA	No 86 BX
No 42 AW	No 217 MW

RCAF Squadron
No 415 GX

RNZAF Squadron
No 487 EG

Left: An early fitting of ASV (air to surface radar detection of vessels) to an early production Beaufort, by heavy style brackets under wings and nose carrying the 'Yagi' aerial arrays. / *IWM*

Below: The officers and men responsible for maintaining the eight effective and three reserve Beauforts of 'A' Flight, No 42 Squadron, late 1941. The squadron had 22 Beauforts of which 16 was the authorised equipment of a standard Beaufort squadron and the remainder reserve aircraft. Normal operating formation was flights of three for patrols, up to four flights of three for major strikes leaving two per flight for immediate reserve. / *via William Webster, Esq*

Out by Beaufort ~ Back by Mosquito

One pilot left Leuchars on December 11, 1941 in a Beaufort and did not return to Britain until over two years later when he touched down at the very same airfield in a Mosquito! This was Flt Lt (later Squadron Leader) Oliver Philpot, MC, DFC, who left on a 'Rover' patrol to the Norwegian coast in Beaufort 'O' of No 42 Squadron.

Sighting a large convoy of ships apparently making for Stavangar, he went low to make sure of his bombs hitting the largest vessel, while his turret gunner blazed away with his machine-gun. The return fire was intense. The Beaufort was hit in the starboard engine and lost height. In spite of a rough sea, Philpot brought his aircraft down to a successful ditching, in which the tail broke completely off aft of the turret. Following the pattern of hangar drills at Leuchars, the four crew members, one injured in the ditching, succeeded in releasing the dinghy from its stowage point in the wing. Luckily the dinghy came away easily. There was controversy over dinghy stowage in Beauforts at this time. The rescue kit had been augmented with medical and food supplies making a greater bulk which was difficult to stow into the space originally designed. The accommodation could not be increased without structural alterations to the wing, so the squadron commander had decided to place all the ancillary items in a separate bag carried inside the aircraft—then in one emergency these had been forgotten by the crew! By the time of Flt Lt Philpot's ditching it had been decided to keep the original kit in the dinghy and the new extras in the cabin.

The crucial action on ditching was for the crew to get clear of the aircraft without delay in case it sank. All four of Philpot's crew kicked themselves clear and bobbed up and down in the swell supported by their Mae West life-jackets. Helping each other into the self-inflating dinghy they awaited events. There was little hope of rescue from Britain. A Beaufort normally did a daily 'Rover' along the southern Norwegian coast but the chances of being seen were remote. They were too distant from Britain and too near the enemy coast to expect air-sea rescue searches, particularly as there had been no time to signal their position before ditching. Night fell and they experienced all the hardships of shipwrecked mariners as they sat cold and cramped in their open dinghy. A Heinkel He115 seaplane in the distance was viewed with apprehension—would the crew signal for their rescue or open fire? As it was, they were apparently not noticed.

On the third day they were picked up by a German warship and taken into Kristiansund, in Norway. Later the crew were split up and sent to various prisoner of war camps in Germany. It was while at Stalag Luft III at Sagan that Philpot, who had been planning escape since capture, had the good fortune to be co-opted into one of the most amazing POW escapes of the war.

The wooden horse escape is now a legend. A vaulting horse was made by the prisoners for exercise and accepted

by the camp staff as a means of keeping the inmates occupied and their minds off escape. But when brought out each day it concealed a prisoner braced against its interior surfaces. Placed always in the same spot, it enabled the hidden prisoner to spend some time each day tunnelling down and along to outside the perimeter wire. A trapdoor covered with the sandy earth of the compound concealed the tunnel entrance.

Eventually three officers escaped from the camp through this tunnel to beyond the perimeter wire. Philpot, taking on the guise of a Norwegian businessman co-operating with the Germans, travelled by rail to Danzig where he stowed away aboard a Swedish ship which sailed for Södertalje near Stockholm. After contacting the British Embassy he was allocated a passage in the bomb-bay of a British Overseas Airways Corporation Mosquito. On loan from the RAF and bearing civil registration, these unarmed Mosquitos flying high and fast at night to evade German fighters over Norway and Denmark, plied mail and returned with limited amounts of important materials, like ball-bearings, between Britain and Stockholm airport. Also, when the occasion arose, a passenger could be carried. This was how Philpot flew back in to Leuchars, over two years after leaving there in his Beaufort.

Above: Beaufort W6537 of No 22 Squadron, loaded with torpedo, being started up at its dispersal pen. / *IWM*

Left: Armed with torpedoes, three of No 86 Squadron's Beaufort Is, set out on a shipping strike. / *IWM*

Below: In other words—'Don't bomb, torpedo or fire at me—I'm neutral!' While German ships were made as inconspicuous as possible, and the movements of Allied ships were notified to Coastal Command areas, there were also neutral ships plying the high seas. They travelled in a blaze of light by night and by day relied on their conspicuous finish and markings to avoid being mistaken for an Allied or Axis ship. The MV *Karmas* shown, of 3 500 tons, was operated by Sweden (Sverige).

23

Meet the Crew

Right: The Beaufort had a crew of four, pilot and observer seen conferring at right, an air gunner and wireless operator, both trained as wireless operator/air gunners. They are wearing Mae West type life-jackets and have parachute packs; when flying they will don flying helmets incorporating earphones like the air gunner at left. All aircrew were volunteers and the minimum aircrew rank was sergeant. / *IWM*

Below: Crew access was by a retractable ladder, then by hand/foot holds to the cabin hatch. While the pilot and observer went through to the nose, the wireless operator took station in the cabin immediately on the left of the hatch with a single port each side for lookout. On the roof of this cabin was the collapsible direction finding loop and fixed VHF aerial. The air gunner went to the right to step into the turret, in this case a Bristol Mk IV with a single Vickers 'K' machine-gun. On the top of the fuselage, behind the turret, is a gas detector paint spot. Of vital importance also was the ground crew: fitters, armourers, flight mechanics, radio and wireless mechanics to mention but a few of the trades involved in maintaining a Beaufort squadron. Coastal airfields were bleak places and a canvas shelter for engine maintenance, as seen left, was essential in inclement weather. Picture taken November 5, 1940. / *IWM*

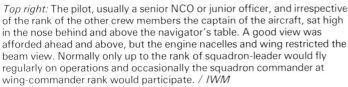

Top right: The pilot, usually a senior NCO or junior officer, and irrespective of the rank of the other crew members the captain of the aircraft, sat high in the nose behind and above the navigator's table. A good view was afforded ahead and above, but the engine nacelles and wing restricted the beam view. Normally only up to the rank of squadron-leader would fly regularly on operations and occasionally the squadron commander at wing-commander rank would participate. / *IWM*

Above right: The observer, sitting in the nose in front of the pilot's controls, was responsible for navigation and observers were renamed navigators in March 1942. Some observers until mid-1941 were actually pilots from an earlier policy that general reconnaissance aircraft should carry two pilots. / *IWM*

Right: Although the Beaufort crew was four, there were five crew stations. For bombing and torpedo run-ins, the observer/navigator left his table seat and took the prone position in the nose to aim and instruct the pilot by R/T on any necessary course correction at this critical stage of an operation. He also had access to a swing seat enabling him to sit by the side of the pilot. / *IWM*

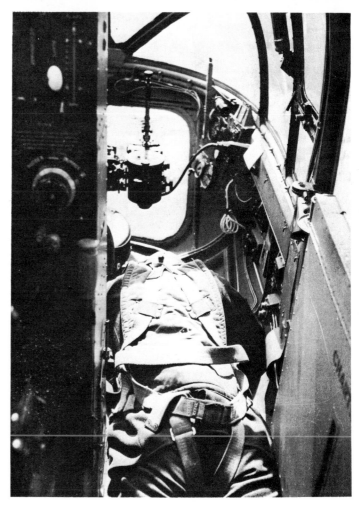

Beauforts and the Break~out.
Chaos in the Channel~ February 12, 1942

The German battle cruisers *Scharnhorst* and *Gneisenau*, accompanied by the cruiser *Prinz Eugen*, passed through the English Channel in daylight on February 12, 1942 under the noses of Royal Navy destroyers, submarines, patrol vessels and motor torpedo boats, the Army's coastal defence guns at Dover, and bombers, fighter-bombers and torpedo-bombers of the Royal Air Force. In addition, there was the gallant, unavailing attack by biplane Swordfish torpedo-bombers of the Fleet Air Arm. The story is well-known. The German ships, under a well co-ordinated air umbrella, put up by the Luftwaffe, got by. This account is concerned with the part the Beauforts played in the operation.

The break-out of the ships was expected. On February 8, 1942 the Commander-in-Chief Coastal Command issued an appreciation titled 'Situation regarding probable break-out of enemy naval forces from Brest'. He actually reported indications that in the past few days the three ships had been exercising in open water and should be ready for sea. Adding information from photographic reconnaissance of a large number of destroyers and E-boats concentrated at Brest, he wrote that it would 'seem to indicate an attempt to force a way up the Channel'.

The document was highly secret. If only security at Coastal Command had been lax, if only there had been careless talk, if only a spy could have filched a copy and conveyed its content to the Germans, the operation might well have been called off. The Germans would not have dared to attempt to force the Channel had they known what the British knew of their intentions.

It cannot be said that the C-in-C Coastal Command was in any way negligent, indeed his counter plans, with the limited forces at his disposal, were as complete as his appreciation was accurate. Dusk to dawn patrols to Brest and night sweeps were instituted, subject to weather. A close co-operation was maintained with Bomber and Fighter Commands. But most important of all was Coastal Command's striking force. The planned use of these was precise:—

'A striking force of a squadron of torpedo-bombers will be maintained at St Eval; a second small striking force of torpedo-bombers will be at Thorney Island. These two forces will be responsible for night work in the Channel. If there is no moon, the reconnaissance aircraft, when they have located the enemy, will be responsible for illuminating the enemy force with flares during the period of the torpedo attack. Co-operation between the torpedo striking forces and the reconnaissance aircraft will be arranged by Nos 19 and 16 Groups. A daylight attack on the enemy force, if it passes successfully through the Straits of Dover, will be carried out by a striking force of torpedo-bombers at present based on Leuchars.'

This was roughly the position four days later when the German warships were passing up the Channel, unobserved until mid-morning in spite of routine patrols. At St Eval, in the South-West, there were 12 Beauforts of Nos 86 and 217 Squadrons on the ground, while three more were in the air sweeping the Bay of Biscay in spite of poor weather. At Thorney Island, the small striking force planned was seven Beauforts of No 217 Squadron. In Scotland the 14 serviceable Beauforts of No 42 Squadron at Leuchars were getting ready to move. They had earlier been ordered south, but their airfield had been snow-bound.

The warships had been spotted first by fighters at 10.42hrs off Le Treport—about 60 miles due south of Dover; well beyond reach of the St Eval Beauforts who had lost their chance of a direct strike. It was past midday before full reaction took place, then there was a sudden welter of activity. The Dover batteries opened fire at 12.18hrs, Dover and Ramsgate motor torpedo boat flotillas attacked, five squadrons of Spitfire VBs took off to escort the six naval Swordfish and only one squadron made contact. From 12.20 onwards further squadrons of Spitfire Vs took off to give withdrawal cover, Hurricane IIB bombers were ordered in to attack enemy escorting vessels and Whirlwinds to escort destroyers going in to attack. In the next thirty minutes, eight Hurricane IICs and 12 Spitfire VBs were ordered to make low-level cannon fire attacks on enemy destroyers which were making smoke to hide the capital ships. This was only a start. Now the Beauforts came on the scene.

By this time the German ships, steaming full out, were getting beyond the range of the Thorney Island squadron. A west-to-east Beaufort switch was put in hand. St Eval Beauforts to Thorney Island, while Thorney Island Beauforts were to go to Manston from where earlier the six Swordfish left, never to return. It had been suggested that the Swordfish should wait until the Thorney Island Beauforts arrived to deliver a co-ordinated attack, but in view of the limited range of the Swordfish, and the rapidly moving German ships, Lt Cdr Esmonde, who received a posthumous VC for leading the attack, decided to set off while he still had a chance of reaching the ships.

At 13.20hrs three more squadrons of Spitfire VCs were scrambled with orders to escort the Thorney Island Beauforts. However, only four of the Beauforts were immediately ready and these took off for Manston, to

Right: A continuous watch was kept on Brest and the positions of the three major German warships carefully noted. In this view of part of the extensive harbour of Brest, intelligence have plotted three points of interest: 1, a new roof to a warehouse damaged in an earlier raid; 2, a Hipper Class cruiser, almost certainly the *Prinz Eugen;* 3, objects on the mole considered to be smoke screen canisters. / *via Sqn Ldr M. Williamson*

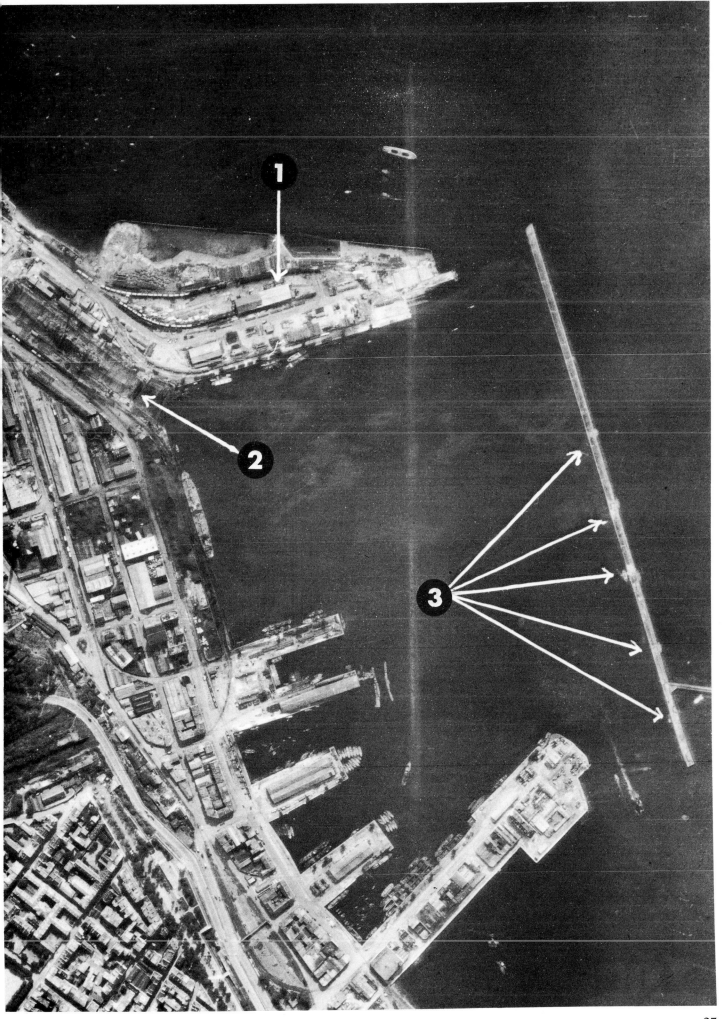

obtain the latest briefing, and to pick up their fighter escort. Approaching Manston they found the airfield such a hive of activity, with aircraft taking-off and landing, that their formation split up as they circled round. Two of the pilots decided to break away and make their way direct to the target area; the other two landed, received briefings and followed. So that instead of a co-ordinated attack, the Beauforts attacked piece-meal and without their planned escorts.

Meanwhile, the other three from Thorney Island reached Manston where they circled—receiving by radio the latest position plots, and they set off to deliver a formation attack. The German ships were picked up on ASV but good visual recognition was not possible because of the smoke screen. The crews decided to attack singly as opportunity presented, but were harassed by enemy fighters and anti-aircraft fire which resulted in the loss of one. As with the earlier attacks, poor visibility precluded observation of results.

No 42 Squadron leaving Leuchars were unaware of the movements of the German warships. Only fourteen of their 22 Beauforts were serviceable for take-off, and only eleven of these had torpedoes, but the remainder, it was thought, could be picked up at their destination—North Coates. But that airfield was snowbound and the Beauforts were diverted to Coltishall, where torpedoes were not available. North Coates was asked to convey them rapidly by road.

Coastal Command HQ were desperately trying to inject some cohesion into the attacks, but having detected the enemy ships so late in their passage, being hampered by snowbound airfields and with bad weather helping to conceal the enemy ships, their hopes were fading. The German ships were rapidly getting out of range and no time could be wasted. Before the extra torpedoes arrived by road at Coltishall, those Beauforts of No 42 Squadron already armed with torpedoes were ordered off to Manston, to rendezvous with Hudsons which would create a diversionary bombing attack.

At last a co-ordinated attack was planned; but again came snags. Two of the Beauforts had engine trouble and could not take-off, so the strike force had dwindled to nine. The Hudson formation was picked up after the Beauforts had waited, circling Manston for thirty minutes. They finally set course for the German ships at 15.34hrs. By that time daylight on that cloudy winter's afternoon was failing and the two formations lost touch.

The Beauforts, on their own, split into two formations; one of six to attack from one side, and three others from the opposite direction. One Beaufort crew, however, got lost in the mist and could not attack and another had a torpedo hang-up. Of the seven torpedo releases, all were seen to be running correctly after dropping, but there was little point in risking damage in the intense anti-aircraft fire to observe results.

Coastal Command pinned their hopes on a final strike. The St Eval Beauforts of Nos 86 and 217 Squadrons on reaching Thorney Island, were sent to strike via Coltishall from where a fighter escort was arranged. The formation commander circling the airfield at 17.00hrs, saw no sign of an escort and, mindful of the approaching dusk, led the twelve aircraft seawards. They swept an area too far southward of ships because of a misleading signal and

Above: Beauforts of No 42 Squadron in formation. / *IWM*

Right: Beauforts of No 86 Squadron setting out. Mk I, AW239, in foreground.

came under fire from German mine-sweepers. By this time it was nearly dark and had started to rain. The Beauforts made their way back, leaving two of their number in the North Sea.

In the final analysis—and there was a most thorough Court of Inquiry—it was difficult to fault the handling of the torpedo-bomber force. They were necessarily dispersed to cover both ends of the Channel and the North Sea with patrols to Norway. There were only three such squadrons. Unit establishment was 16 aircraft plus six reserve so that only 48 Beauforts were on immediate call, but only 33 were serviceable and therefore flyable. Of these three did not have torpedoes and a further two went unserviceable, leaving 28 that actually set out to strike. Of these 13 failed to find the ships, three were shot down and one had a torpedo hang-up, so that only 11 of the 48 are known to have launched torpedoes that day; it is, however, possible that those shot down did attack.

Beaufort crew training was questioned, not in a way that disparaged the efforts of the crews but by suggesting that a very high standard of training was necessary for torpedo attacks, which it was difficult to attain in war. The need for a faster, longer-range torpedo-bomber was pressed and Bristol had this in hand with the Torbeau—the torpedo-carrying version of the Beaufighter.

The Beaufort Gains Reliability. Introduction of the Beaufort II 1941~42

As early as April 17, 1941 an Air Ministry Order advised the Royal Air Force that 'certain Beaufort aeroplanes will be fitted with Pratt & Whitney Twin Wasp S3C4-G engines. This type of Beaufort will be known as Beaufort II'. These engines had first been fitted to N1110 to test in England the power unit of the Beauforts being built in Australia.

Because of the complaints of the Taurus engines, it was decided early in 1941 to fit the Beaufort with Twin Wasps, and the production change-over was effected in the autumn. The first, AW244, flew in September and deliveries to the RAF started that month. The Twin Wasps did little for the Beaufort in the way of performance; the maximum speed unloaded was raised by 5mph to 265mph; the service ceiling, not a vital factor for a low-level bomber, was also raised but range was reduced from 1 600 to 1 450 miles. The saving grace was the fact that this Beaufort type did not have engines with a bad reputation.

The delivery of Beaufort IIs to squadrons did little to improve operational efficiency. On the night of January 6/7, 1942, Beauforts of No 42 Squadron, joined with Hudsons of Nos 28 and 608 Squadrons in attacking shipping at Bergen. Two of the Beauforts left Wick at 02.20hrs, but neither reached the target area, aircraft 'V' did find a 1 500 ton ship at the northern end of Hjelte Fjord and dropped bombs, but results could not be observed as the defences came to life, firing at the aircraft from across the fjord. Shortly after 04.00hrs, three more of No 42's Beauforts took off singly from Leuchars; 'M' and 'R' failed to find the target, while 'E' met a night fighter over Kors Fjord and was forced to jettison its bombs to assist evasion.

A daylight attack on January 17 was made by No 86 Squadron on shipping at St Peter Port, Guernsey. The main objective was a jetty with a 6 000 ton ship on one side and two smaller vessels on the other. The Beauforts made a low approach in line astern at 11.00hrs, aircraft 'B' so low and close that it was nearly hit by 'Q's bombs, and actually flew between the masts of the largest ship. Their bombs, all with 11-second fuses, burst diagonally across the jetty. Sweeping low over St Julian's Pier a party of thirty men wearing steel helmets was attacked with machine-guns, as were others seen on Castle Pier. A party parading in a courtyard were seen to break ranks and scatter.

One of the early Mk IIs, AW271, was involved in a most tragic accident on April 30, 1942. It was being used by the Coastal Command Development Unit at Ballykelly for

testing the parachuting of a wounded man from a Beaufort by static line. This method assumed that the wounded man would be unconscious or wounded in the arms, and unable to pull the release ring of his parachute. The idea was that his comrades would attach a static line and his parachute would be pulled open when he fell clear of the aircraft. A test drop was made, watched from the ground. The horrified observers saw the parachutist drop, hang, then the parachute opened and was swept by the slipstream onto the tail of the aircraft. Control was so affected that AW271 spun in and was burnt out before any of the three aboard could use their own parachute properly.

Less than a month later a complete No 86 Squadron crew was killed after returning from an operational patrol while actually circling Wick in AW345 waiting to land. They hit the 200ft high wireless mast on top of a 400ft hill near Wick.

Unfortunately the supply of Twin Wasps was not assured because of sinkings of merchant ships from America and after the 165th Beaufort II, production had to be switched back to the Taurus engines. These were, however, the later and improved Mk XII and XV versions. Other improvements that were incorporated on the production line included Bristol BI Mk V turrets and ASV became a standard fitting. Youngman pneumati

Left: The second production Beaufort II AW245 seen at Filton in August 1941, was the first Mk II in service and reached No 217 Squadron in November. In February 1942 this aircraft was damaged in action and after repair by Folland Ltd it served with No 5 OTU. Although involved in an accident at Long Kesh in November 1942, it survived again until August 1945 when it was written off as deteriorated beyond use. / *Bristol Aeroplane Company*

Top left: The Mk II form. Apart from the change to Pratt & Whitney Twin Wasp S3C4-G, various refinements that had been incorporated over the years were embodied in the Mk II. These included a new type direction-finding loop in a plastic fairing over the cabin top, ASV installed as a standard fitting with 'Yagi' aerials under fuselage chin, port and starboard wings. Strangely, in spite of the little use made of the chin gun positions, this became a standard production fit. / *Bristol Aeroplane Company*

Above: Early production Mk II Beauforts still had the original Bristol Mk IV turret. This mounted a single .303 Vickers 'K' type machine-gun. Some were later modified to Mk IE to take two 'K' guns; an experimental Mk II version of turret to take two .303 Brownings did not reach production. / *Bristol Aeroplane Company*

Centre left: Some late production Mk I Beauforts, such as DD954 illustrated, had a refinement denied early Mk IIs. This was a Blenheim-type turret, the Bristol B1 type in its Mk V form to take two .303 Browning guns. / *Bristol Aeroplane Company*

dive-brakes were introduced, but did not prove successful in service. They were usually kept locked in their up position and were later removed.

During 1942 the Beaufort went out of squadron service in the United Kingdom, and their role was taken over by Beaufighters, while the existing squadrons took their aircraft east. There was, however, some minor and one large-scale operation before the Beauforts left.

Birds in Beauforts ~ A Pigeon on 'Ops'~ February 1942

On many operations, Beauforts had a fifth crew-member—a pigeon. They were signed for like parachutes, and taken in a basket for the duration of a 'trip' and returned on landing. Coastal Command stations such as Thorney Island and Leuchars had pigeon training sections, their pigeons coming from the 200 000 pigeons given to the British Services during the Second World War by racing pigeon breeders, through the National Pigeon Service.

When Beaufort 'I', L9965, of No 42 Squadron left to patrol the Norwegian coast on February 23, 1942, the pilot, Sqn Ldr W. M. Cliff, and his crew took aboard a pigeon. This was brought by the wireless operator, who was responsible for all forms of signalling and on this day he signed out NEHU. 40. NS1, a blue chequered hen that had been bred by Mr A. R. Colley of Whitburn, Sunderland and trained by Messrs Ross and Norrie of Long Lane, Broughty Ferry, Angus, Scotland.

The patrol off Norway was uneventful, but on return one engine stopped at 17.30hrs. Unable to maintain height on the other engine, the pilot was forced to ditch and the aircraft partially broke-up on hitting the sea. The crew quickly launched their dinghy and boarded it but did not have time to get the pigeon out and send a message.

At 18.00hrs that day the RAF duty officer at Leuchars notified the Air-Sea Rescue Service that the Beaufort was overdue and that they had been in touch with it when it was 168 miles east of Aberdeen. Catalina 'K' of No 413 (RCAF) Squadron was setting out from Sullom Voe later in the evening for a night patrol and this area was included on her patrol track.

Throughout the next morning from first light, Hudsons 'F', 'K', 'H' & 'P' of No 320 (Dutch) Squadron and Blenheims 'H', 'S', & 'X' of No 489 (New Zealand) Squadron, also based at Leuchars, set out at intervals. Each one flew on a different bearing to comb the area.

Meanwhile, a plumber at Broughty Ferry found his pigeon, allotted to Leuchars, back in the cote having arrived soon after dawn, exhausted, wet and oily. RAF Leuchars was telephoned and Sergeant Davidson of the Pigeon Service arrived, and confirmed it was the pigeon booked out on 'Ops' Beaufort 'I' deducing from the condition of the bird that its basket had burst in the crash, freeing the bird and throwing it in to the oily water. Taking into account the time of the last message and that the pigeon would not fly at night, he estimated the crash was nearer than 168 miles and on his advice the search pattern was changed.

At 11.06hrs Hudson 'H' of No 320 (Dutch) Squadron sent out a sighting report; the dinghy was sighted 90 miles east of the Firth of Forth. Within 30 minutes high speed rescue launches HSL118 and HSL158 were leaving Blyth, followed by HSL137 and HSL157 from Aberdeen. To maintain touch, Beauforts of No 42 Squadron flew locating flights at intervals as a navigational exercise. The Navy, wishing to play its part, sent out Walruses W9K and W9L from Arbroath to effect a pick-up, and the RAF then added Beaufighters 'D' & 'T' of No 248 Squadron, another Leuchars-based squadron, to give fighter cover. As it was, the Blyth HSLs were in the best position to effect a pick-up and the four survivors were brought safely home.

The crew gave a dinner in honour of the pigeon and her trainer. They nick-named the pigeon *Winkie* as she appeared to be winking at them, but this unusually slow reaction of the eyelid was possibly the after effects of extreme fatigue. The bird was awarded the Dickin medal.

Above right: The Army Pigeon Service operated by the Royal Signals supplied hundreds of birds for operational use in RAF Bomber and Coastal Command, including Beauforts on sea patrols. The message container is seen here being fixed to the pigeon's leg. / *Courtesy The Racing Pigeon Publishing Co*

Left: To help allay pilot fatigue on long patrols the Beaufort was fitted with an auto-pilot. It seldom worked. Even when serviceable it was too dangerous to use at the Beaufort's usual very low operating height. / *IWM*

Right: A Beaufort II on a training patrol.

Sink the Prinz.
February ~ May 1942

The *Prinz Eugen* after escaping through the Channel on Febuary 15, made a surprising re-appearance. At 11.10hrs on February 21, nine days after the escape, she was seen off the Dutch coast in company with the pocket battleship *Admiral von Scheer,* making towards the Channel. The Beaufort force were alerted; it appeared they were to have a second chance. Again the weather was bad and searching aircraft failed to find the ships which had made a feint and then, cloaked by the weather, turned about and made for Norway—their planned destination. But next day a Royal Navy submarine managed to put a torpedo into the *Prinz Eugen* and cripple her.

Temporary repairs were made to the cruiser at Trondheim, taking two months, sufficient for her to attempt to return to Germany for dockyard repairs. A photographic reconnaissance report received at Coastal Command Headquarters at 16.30hrs on May 16, 1942, brought the vital intelligence that a cruiser, preceded by two destroyers, was off Trondheim steaming south-west at high speed. The Beaufort force was immediately alerted; they were to have a third chance at hitting the *Prinz Eugen.*

Estimating that the warships would pass Stadlandet around midnight, 14 Beauforts were despatched an hour before midnight with crews briefed to search the area. All returned, having failed completely to locate the force. Meanwhile, six Hampdens had been further south to the Haugessund area to sow mines in the presumed path of the ships.

Throughout the next day, relays of reconnaissance aircraft kept the area under surveillance until two differently timed sighting reports gave the crucial speed and course assessment for a strike mission. It was by then early evening. At 17.00hrs Coastal Command signalled the strike orders to No 18 Group, specifying that all available Beauforts, with an escort of Beaufighters and high-flying Hudsons as a diversion, would strike at the force in the Lister area, south of Stavanger.

No 18 Group had already made plans from earlier alerts. They were rather more subtle about decoys than their Command HQ. The Lister area was within Blenheim range and this aircraft, progenitor of the Beaufort, was much more likely to be confused with Beauforts than the tubby, twin-finned Hudsons.

Within an hour of the signal, the first wave of the force was on its way, heading for Kristiansund from where they would sweep back along the estimated route of the warships, now known to be the *Prinz Eugen* and four destroyers. In this wave were 12 Beauforts of No 42 Squadron, six Blenheim IVCs of No 404 (RCAF) Squadron, and four Beaufighters—two each from Nos 235 and 248 Squadrons.

A late reconnaissance report gave a more precise position. Signalled to the aircraft *en route* it resulted in a course change—and a sighting. As pre-arranged, the

Beaufighters went straight in, raking the destroyers with cannon-fire to disrupt their protective anti-aircraft fire in the Beauforts' interests. The Blenheims, meanwhile, occupied themselves in dummy runs giving the impression of torpedo attacks to distract the defences further, and then in bravely engaging some Messerschmitt Bf109s that came on the scene.

The Beauforts were in two waves of six aircraft. Each wave divided into sections of two for the attack, with a leader and a follower. The object was to take into account each change of course the *Prinz Eugen* might make to evade the torpedoes. So intense was the anti-aircraft fire, in spite of the diversionary efforts, that the first three leader aircraft were shot down before dropping their torpedoes. The remaining nine released their torpedoes between 1 800 and 4 000 yards from the cruiser.

As one Beaufort pilot reported: 'At 20.14hrs saw one cruiser and four destroyers whilst still in formation with other Beauforts. Leader altered course to starboard and we went in to attack. Aircraft was attacked by one Me109 which missed owing to my evasive action in turning to port. Immediately afterwards dropped torpedo at cruiser, which presented a very good target, and a hit was thought probable. Aircraft was then hit by flak and partially disabled, as a shell-burst on the stern frame damaged the elevator controls and rudder controls. Aircraft could not turn and was very difficult to handle.

'At 20.19hrs aircraft was attacked by three Me109s, one of which was driven away by a Beaufighter. The second Messerschmitt turned and the third closed in to attack. The rear gunner was dazed by a hit on the turret, and the wireless operator took his place until he recovered four or five minutes later. Enemy aircraft was shooting low and was not keen to close in with our aircraft, which should have been an easy target, as no evasive action was possible. Wireless operator claimed several hits on this enemy aircraft'.

Although it was damaged in the tail and around the

turret by cannon shells and machine-gun fire, the pilot nursed his aircraft 300 miles across the sea and made a successful crash landing.

A second wave of fifteen Beauforts from No 86 Squadron escorted by Beaufighters had followed. Unfortunately a reporting error sent them too far north of the German warships and, in a coastal sweep to locate the ships, they were intercepted by a strong force of Bf109s. The Beauforts kept formation to mass their defensive fire—such as it was. Their crews claimed that five Bf109s were destroyed, but four of the Beauforts were lost and of the 11 remaining, seven were forced to jettison their torpedoes.

This was the last of the major actions by Beauforts based in Britain. No 42 Squadron ceased operations that month in preparation to moving east and No 86 Squadron flew their Beauforts to the Middle East, while the ground crew was reduced to cadre.

The threat from German surface ships was receding. The *Prinz Eugen* made Kiel but was in dock some time following earlier damage from a submarine torpedo attack. (She was finally sunk by an atom bomb in postwar Bikini Atoll nuclear tests.)

Top left: Load with torpedo. Armourers adjusting the drum control for lowering the torpedo while an electrician checks the control system. The air tail was fitted to stabilise the weapon during its drop. An earlier experiment tried on Beauforts was the winged Toraplane project and in 1941 a Beaufort modified for this project was kept under canvas at Leuchars, but never used. The British Mk XII was the standard torpedo for Beaufort strikes, but practice drops were with special torpedoes. / *IWM*

Right: A No 86 Squadron Beaufort II flying in the vicinity of Ben Nevis during 1942. / *IWM*

Top right: Training went on all the time — a Beaufort I of an Operational Training Unit. / *IWM*

The Shift East 1941~1943

As the war progressed, so the sphere of Beaufort operations shifted east. By 1943 there were no Beauforts operational in North-West Europe, by 1944 there were no Beauforts operational in the Mediterranean or Middle East areas and in 1945 the Beaufort was only operational in the Far East.

Beauforts were sent east from July 1941 and No 39 Squadron received its first in August 1941, but since it was only a trickle at first the squadron did not completely discard its Marylands until 1942. The squadron was engaged mainly on convoy attacks from advanced bases in North Africa. A detachment from the squadron later went to Malta and for the remainder of the war frequently shuttled from Malta to North Africa and vice versa. The squadron's first major success came on January 23, 1942 when a 20-ship convoy was attacked and one large merchantman was crippled.

There followed a general shift of Beaufort squadrons from the United Kingdom eastwards. In March 1942 No 22, the very first Beaufort squadron, was the first to move east. Originally intended for Singapore, their destination was changed to Ceylon but because of the situation in the Desert war, they were held temporarily for operations in North Africa.

No 217 Squadron was next to receive an overseas posting. In May 1942 the ground echelon were shipped to the Far East while the Beauforts flew out via Malta the following month and were retained on the island for operations until August and never did rejoin their ground crews who arrived in Ceylon in July and were used for Hudson maintenance. Also detailed for the Far East was No 42 Squadron which left Scotland after a two-year stay in June 1942. Finally, No 86 Squadron left Scotland in July for the Middle East. A flight of No 86, together with a flight of No 217, joined the flight of No 39 Squadron at Malta to bring the last-named squadron up to strength.

These squadrons were to suffer losses in operations and training, and a steady flow of replacements was necessary; it was also necessary to form training units overseas. At the time there was a steady flow of Hudsons and Blenheims eastward, so that Beauforts were fed into the normal pattern of forwarding.

There were three main transit streams. Some aircraft were crated after leaving the production line, shipped from Bristol or Birkenhead, destined for a Maintenance Unit overseas. Others flew out via Gibraltar, Malta and Suez Canal Zone. There was an intermediate way of Beauforts being shipped crated to Takoradi in West Africa, where they were assembled and flown across Africa to Egypt.

Those Beauforts that flew out were normally processed through the Maintenance Unit at Kemble and taken on strength by the Overseas Aircraft Despatch Unit. It was logical that the departure airfield for the long haul over the sea to Gibraltar should be on Britain's south-western

tip; this was Portreath, near Redruth, in Cornwall.

As related earlier, the Beaufort had a poor performance on one engine and an engine failure on overseas ferrying could be fatal. Two of the first Beauforts to fly out, N1034 and AW201 on March 30th, 1942 failed to reach Malta; and one that did reach Malta on April 14 was wrecked before its engines stopped. While taxying off the runway at Luqa, AW282 was shot up by two BF109s killing one and injuring four RAF men. Also that month Sgt T. J. H. Mitchell and his crew in AW388 were all killed in transit. In many cases the reason was not known, although L9893 provided a clue when it limped to Malta on June 10 with a crew member killed by a Bf109 attack 60 miles off Cape Bon. Five days later DD975 disappeared. Some like AW274 didn't even start! This aircraft crashed into a Whirlwind before leaving Portreath.

Several Beauforts disappeared *en route* in August, DD932 and DD953 on successive days. That month JM513, destined for India, crash-landed in Portugal; another crew that landed DW894 intact near Lisbon, after running short of fuel, set the Beaufort alight and marched off to report to the British Embassy. But these losses were less than 10 per cent of the whole. By the end of the year over a hundred had reached their Middle East destinations.

The loss rate percentage was higher for overseas transit

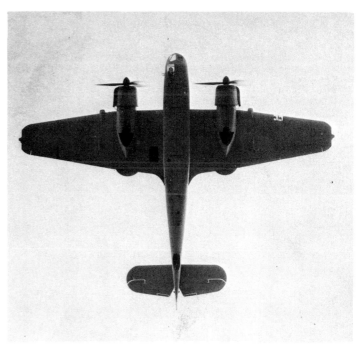

han on operations. Two measures were taken to reduce losses in transit. Special courses for transit crews and alternative transit. During October a large number of Beauforts were prepared to convoy to Takoradi and sailed from Birkenhead in two convoys during October 1942. Both convoys were attacked by German U-boats in the Atlantic off West Africa. On October 29 the MV *Primrose Hill* of 7 628 tons carrying six Beauforts (DW808, DW857, DW860, DW863, DW864 and DW866) was sunk, as was the MV *Wallsend* of 3 157 tons torpedoed on December 2 with DW859, DW865 and DW867 to DW869 aboard. So more Beauforts were sunk by submarines than submarines were sunk by Beauforts in spite of its subsidiary anti-submarine role.

Beauforts despatched by other ships reached Takoradi in the Gold Coast (now Ghana) where they were uncrated, re-assembled, tested and convoyed with a navigational aircraft across the West African reinforcement route to the Chad, onward to the Sudan and then the last 1 000 miles northward to Cairo.

Flying out all the way was the most economical and time-saving method and after No 301 Ferry Unit had been formed to give some training in the UK to all crews flying out East, a few Beaufort crews were fitted in. But No 301 could not meet the demand in late 1942, so No 306 Ferry Unit was formed in January 1943 tasked initially with the

Above left: No 22 Squadron, seen here setting out on a strike, were the first of the squadrons to move overseas. / *IWM*

Top right: Improved form of late production Beaufort Is evinced by EK982 seen at Filton in 1942 with forward-firing guns in the nose, tropical filter on Taurus XVI engines, streamlined D/F cover on fuselage top, ASV 'yagi' aerials under port wing and front fuselage, and Bristol B1 Mk V turret. / *Bristol Aeroplane Company*

Above right: The Beaufort's form. To improve the stability of the early Taurus-engined versions, local extensions, made of sheet dural, were fitted to the mainplane trailing edges, giving a peculiar bulge to the wing shape aft of the engine nacelles. The transparent covers to the navigational lights in the wingtips, and landing lights in the port wing leading edge, both give an apparent distortion to the wingshape. This photo also provides a unique view of the perspex floor of the prone position in the nose.

training and preparation of 25 Beaufort ferry crews. This entailed Beaufort handling under supervision, navigation, special briefings, kitting out and inoculations.

So from 1941 to well into 1943, there was a steady traffic of Beauforts leaving the UK for places East. The Middle East collecting point was Shallufa on the Suez Canal, a few miles north of Port Suez, where a Beaufort pool was established. Another was at Jodhpur in India.

Maltese Mêlée
June 15, 1942

After the loss of Greece and Crete, and Rommel's advance along the North African coast, the importance of the Malta base in thwarting Axis aspirations in the Mediterranean became paramount. To bring relief and sustain forces on the island, now in desperate need of supplies, it was decided to run two simultaneous convoys, one from Britain via Gibraltar approaching from the West and one from Alexandria in the East. It was to be expected that the Italian fleet would not miss this opportunity to play its part in starving the island into submission. With most of the available British warships tied up with convoy protection, there had to be another counter—Beaufort torpedo-bombers.

Malta was crowded in early June 1942. With a recent influx from a carrier of 59 Spitfires there were now 100 of these fighters. To supplement the small strike and reconnaissance force on the island, six torpedo-carrying Wellingtons of No 38 Squadron, six Baltimores of No 69 Squadron and the fifteen Beaufighters of No 235 Squadron were flown in. To share the few cratered and wreckage-strewn airfields available with all the other aircraft came fourteen Beauforts of No 217 Squadron, veterans from Coastal Command.

Spitfires on reconnaissance over enemy ports late on June 14, brought evidence from their photographs that units of the Italian fleet were at sea, and Wellingtons went out throughout the night dropping flares to reveal their whereabouts. A sighting report from a Wellington at 02.00hrs led to the Beaufort squadron being alerted for a dawn strike. Immediately there was feverish activity. Crews sleeping in the tunnels and shelters were awakened for preparation and briefing. The aircraft were of necessity widely dispersed—a vital precaution for torpedo-laden aircraft on an airfield under regular enemy attack.

Wing Commander Davis led his force 200 miles to the east where the two battleships, two cruisers and seven destroyers sighted was the greatest array of enemy ships that had ever been presented to Beaufort crews. As was to be expected, the Italian fleet sent up a tremendous anti-aircraft barrage, altered course and put up a smoke screen. The Beauforts attacked from different directions and claimed hits on both capital ships. They crippled the cruiser *Trento* with two hits and the commander of the British submarine P35, shadowing the force, watched the attack and took the opportunity to sink her.

The only other Beaufort unit then operating in the Mediterranean was No 39 Squadron which had just received some of the first Mk IIs. Because of Rommel's advance they had been moved back eastwards, so that the

Maintenance in Malta—a Beaufort undergoes servicing on the island. A feature of Beaufort Is operating in the Near and Middle East was the special Vokes air filter mounted on top of the Taurus engine cowling. /IWM

Indicative of maintenance on Malta is the effort to conserve fuel. An airman, left, holds a tin to collect seepage from the fuel jettison pipe which can be used in military vehicles on the island then under siege. / *IWM*

Italian ships were outside their normal radius of action. At this stage Headquarters RAF, Middle East, gave a magnificent example of staff work with the shortest possible delay. Before the No 217 Squadron Beauforts had returned from their attack, twelve of No 39 Squadron's Beauforts were winging their way towards the same target, flying in four vees of three each, their crews briefed to attack and carry on to Malta as they would not have fuel to return. HQ ME had arranged for a Maryland to send out 'Rooster' signals to home them on to the target area, and even a diversion had been arranged. Five Liberators of No 160 Squadron, staging on their way to India, had been held and detailed to co-ordinate a high-level bombing attack simultaneous with the torpedo attack. They were to be joined at the same time by Liberators of the Halverson Detachment, USAAF—B-24s temporarily in the Middle East after an attack on the Ploesti oilfields in Romania.

But the enemy, too, had reacted promptly and as the Beauforts neared their target they were intercepted by Messerschmitt Bf109s. They attacked the rearmost vee formation coming in from the beam, diving and turning to attack from directly behind. In spite of increasing speed and weaving, two Beauforts were shot down. Two others with damaged airframes and wounded wireless operators were forced to turn away and make directly for Malta. Putting on extra boost had caused abnormally high fuel consumption and three more had to turn away, one of which ended up in enemy territory.

Five were left. Fortunately all went well. The 'Rooster' homing worked effectively and the Beauforts were brought within three miles and a visual sighting of their target. Simultaneously the Liberators from their Suez bases were approaching and the Italian fleet, confused by the high-flying threat, turned to present themselves broadside on to the low-flying Beauforts. Both attacks scored hits, but the Italian ships were not stopped and the Alexandria convoy had to turn back. The five Beauforts then struggled to make Malta, two badly damaged; of these one made a belly landing and the other swung on touch-down, slewed

off the runway, hit a wrecked aircraft and caught fire—the crew escaped injury. The other three landed safely.

While these two strikes had been taking place in the Ionian Sea, sighting reports had been received of more Italian ships menacing the other Allied convoy approaching from the West. Only two Beauforts with rather inexperienced crews had remained on the ground, but these with four naval Albacore biplane torpedo-bombers made up a scratch strike force and set out at 09.00hrs before the others returned. Sixteen Spitfires were sent out as escort and were needed to ward off long-range Bf109s which jettisoned their tanks and came in to attack. The first Beaufort crew claimed a hit on a cruiser and the second went in to 300 yards before dropping. The damage caused was not great, but the attack can be deemed most successful, for although the Allied convoy was to suffer more air attacks, the surface threat was lifted when the Italian warships returned to port.

Now, two Beaufort squadrons were concentrated on Malta and were held on standby. During the afternoon, it was decided to mount a strike by No 217 Squadron at dusk. This proved abortive for a number of reasons. The crews were tired after continuous action and standby, they met with unexpected head-winds and a navigational error was made. Moreover, the crews were unaccustomed to night flying and special reception arrangements had to be made at Malta. The Beaufort wireless operators were given direction-finding priority and airfield floodlighting at Luqa was supplemented by Army searchlights. All landed safely. The Beauforts' most intensive day of action was over. The enemy warships had, however, achieved their purpose, for the relieving convoy from Alexandria was forced to turn back.

A typical home-based Beaufort I of 1941 in temperate sea scheme camouflage, serving with No 86 Squadron of RAF Coastal Command.

Top left: The Beaufort prototype as delivered in natural metal finish in October 1938 from the Filton works of the Bristol Aeroplane Company. Its main undercarriage wheels retracted backward and upwards and the tailwheel forward and upwards, but in service, for a period, a tailwheel modification to prevent tailwheel shimmying required the tailwheel to be non-retracting.

Below left: A Beaufort I of No 22 Squadron RAF with blackened undersurfaces, bestowed on occasions for a series of night torpedo, mining or bombing operations. Portrayed here in 1941 armed with a torpedo, this aircraft has sheet dural extensions to the wing trailing edge aft of the engine nacelles, fitted as a service modification to improve stability.

Top right: A Beaufort I of No 42 Squadron RAF in the original temperate land scheme camouflage given to early production aircraft. Based at Leuchars in 1941, this particular aircraft was flown by Flying Officer A. K. Passmore. Later in the year the code letters AW were painted white in a new styling to render them more conspicuous.

Above: One of the few Beauforts to serve in Canada, Mk I N1005 flew at No 32 Operational Conversion Unit located at Patricia Bay, British Columbia, operated by the Royal Canadian Air Force. The original temperate land scheme camouflage, bestowed on production in 1940, was retained at least until late 1941.

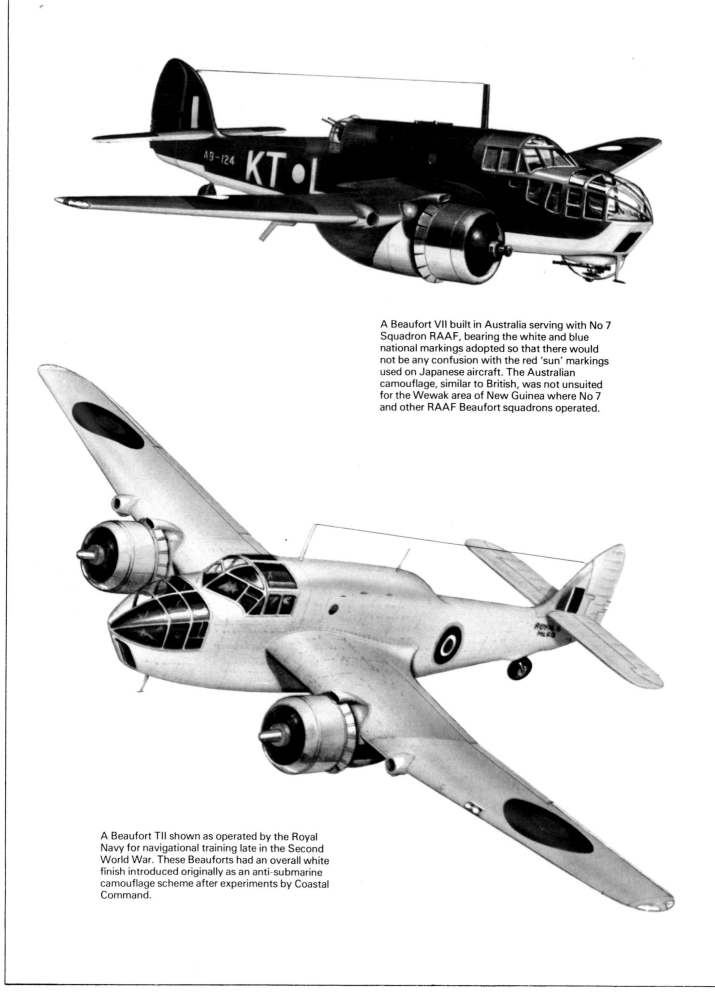

A Beaufort VII built in Australia serving with No 7 Squadron RAAF, bearing the white and blue national markings adopted so that there would not be any confusion with the red 'sun' markings used on Japanese aircraft. The Australian camouflage, similar to British, was not unsuited for the Wewak area of New Guinea where No 7 and other RAAF Beaufort squadrons operated.

A Beaufort TII shown as operated by the Royal Navy for navigational training late in the Second World War. These Beauforts had an overall white finish introduced originally as an anti-submarine camouflage scheme after experiments by Coastal Command.

Anti~Afrika Korps

Malta's Beauforts were continually on the alert during the summer of 1942. On June 21 eight of 217 Squadron's Beauforts sent out to attack a convoy, found a destroyer and several merchant vessels steaming in line astern. Anti-aircraft fire was intense and claimed Squadron Leader Lynn and his crew, leading the attack, and two other Beauforts. Another, hit by shell splinters, was brought back by a wounded pilot. Hits were observed, and the German MV *Reichenfels* of 7 744 tons was sunk.

Two days later seven of No 217's Beauforts were accompanied by five of No 39's to the toe of Italy where four destroyers and two merchant ships were attacked at the cost of two 39 Squadron aircraft and crews and one of 217 Squadron which was brought back by Sgt Nolon, although he was wounded in the leg, to crash on landing.

As a result of the losses, a close examination of tactics was made. In the months to come a set daylight attack scheme was worked out. The Beauforts would set out in three vics of three aircraft in arrowhead formation, and form up with their escort. Four Beaufighters would fly with the Beauforts at sea level, weaving on their flanks, two more acting as anti-aircraft fire decoys with four others as top cover would fly some two miles astern.

The approach to the target was made to a point estimated two hours' steaming ahead, where the formation would turn to meet the flotilla or convoy head-on. The top cover would climb to 3 000 feet while the Beauforts rose to 300 feet. Four miles from the target the Beauforts would deploy to attack from different directions on the flanks, while the anti-flak Beaufighters went straight ahead to shoot up the escorts. A post-attack rendezvous was arranged about eight miles astern. If fighters threatened, the Beauforts would bunch together to concentrate fire-power and keep low to prevent aircraft attacking from the blind spot beneath the tail.

A convoy off the Greek coast brought 12 No 217 Beauforts out from Luqa at 06.45 on July 31, with a Beaufighter escort. Failing to find the ships they returned at mid-day and No 39 took over the task at last light. They found eight destroyers escorting three merchant vessels. A ship was hit, but not sunk. Two Beauforts failed to return and Squadron Leader Gibbs crashed on landing his damaged aircraft.

On July 21 there was a mixed strike. No 86 Squadron's crews had arrived at Malta from the United Kingdom. Four of their Beauforts, with three of No 217 Squadron's, led by two from No 39 Squadron including Squadron Leader Gibbs, attacked a convoy off Cephalonia. Three days later, when six Beauforts, three each from Nos 217 and 86 Squadrons, attacked two destroyers and an E-boat escorting the 6 340 ton Italian MV *Vettor Pisani,* the whole of the No 86 Squadron formation was shot down on the run in. By a combination of both torpedo and bomb hits the vessel was sunk. For this reason the same mixture was used four days later, when 217 Squadron sent out three Beauforts with bombs and the same number with torpedoes. The remaining aircraft of No 86 Squadron were absorbed by No 39 Squadron and No 86 no longer existed as a separate Beaufort squadron, and No 217 Squadron moved to the Far East.

Attacks continued as the Axis tried to sustain their troops in North Africa. No 39 Squadron was withdrawn

Evidence of the success of the anti-shipping campaign to deny supplies to the Africa Korps, is shown by this picture of Benghazi harbour after re-capture by the Allies. / *IWM*

from October 1 to Landing Ground 228, 30 miles behind the front in North Africa. The object was to prevent supplies reaching Tobruk from Crete 350 miles across the Mediterranean. Due to their patrols and strikes the Axis were forced to use Benghazi entailing a much longer road haul to the front.

Another Beaufort Squadron, No 47, started anti-submarine and convoy escort duties from Shandur on October 8. They were joined for a short period by No 42 Squadron staging through on their way to the East. On November 1 three of No 47's Beauforts took on a convoy of vital supplies for Rommel in the Gulf of Bomba near Tobruk. Ignoring the destroyer escort in preference to attacking the tanker, they saw one torpedo run straight at the ship and score a direct hit followed by a terrific explosion in which the whole ship disintegrated. Eighteen days later the Squadron lost their CO, Wg Cdr R. A. Sprague, who crashed on a communications flight in DE118.

After the El Alamein battle and the rolling back of Rommel's forces, Tobruk and Benghazi were so damaged that there was little further point in the enemy using them. In consequence in November No 42 Squadron continued on their way to the Far East and No 39 went back to Malta to join the other Beauforts there. Plans were for the island to maintain a torpedo strike force of 22 Beauforts, and two support squadrons of Beaufighters, on standby to attack the Italian fleet expected to intervene in a new series of convoys to Malta.

In spite of alarms, there were no further attacks on enemy fighting ships, but several attacks on merchant vessels. Once the convoys had arrived and the fuel supply was again assured, torpedo rovers by day and moonlight were instituted, and a mining programme covering Tripoli, Tunis, Bizerta and Palermo was carried out.

Moonlight searches were made when the moon was between 20 to 40 degrees above the horrizon. Then, taking a 200-mile coastal strip, three Beauforts would fly at 4, 7 and 10 miles offshore with all crew members searching up the moonpath.

Room had to be made at Luqa for a Wellington bomber wing in connection with the fighting now going on in Tripolitania after the North African landings, as it was the only suitable night flying base on Malta. Now that the Eighth Army had rolled Rommel back across Libya, there were plenty of airfields in North Africa and No 39, leaving a flight of six at Malta moved to Shallufa, Berka and then Gambut. Mining continued to be carried out, but there were fewer strikes and an amount of training was ordered for new crews.

By now the majority of Beauforts overseas were Mk IIs and the Wasp engines were proving far more reliable than the Taurus. The few Mk Is were used reluctantly on training. A brake with a Ferodo lining on the tail-wheel had superseded the tail-wheel lock and proved very efficient; this change, with a high standard of maintenance on the main wheel brakes minimised swinging after landing.

As the battle in North Africa rolled westward, so Malta increased in importance as a base for strike aircraft and No 39 Squadron rejoined their single flight there in January 1943. Malta was now stronger than it had ever been.

Right: Dark undersurfaces for this Beaufort, believed of No 39 Squadron, on Malta, to render it unconspicuous for night attacks on Italian ports and enemy occupied harbours in North Africa. Even the white of the roundel was darkened, but the yellow roundel outline ring remained. The cowlings have been specially whitened as a visual warning to ground crews on night handling to beware of the propellers. / IWM

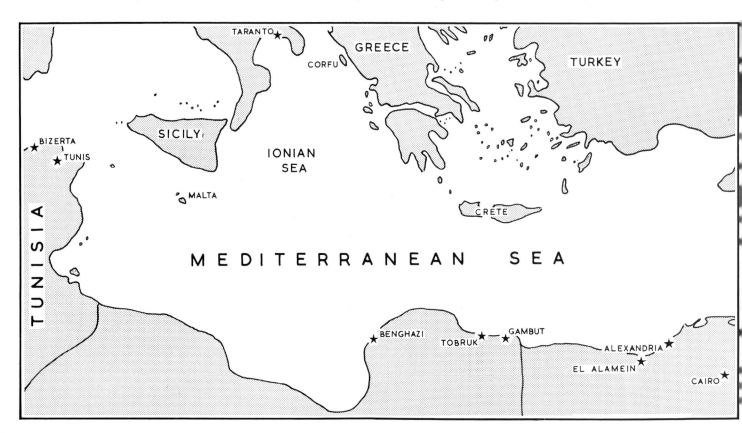

Out by Beaufort ~ Back by Cant

During operations off the west coast of Greece, when Beauforts of No 217 Squadron were making a low-level attack on a convoy stealing along the coast, one pilot, dissatisfied with his run-in, circled round for a second run. It was tempting fate. The crew had the satisfaction of seeing their torpedo run true before their aircraft was hit and forced to ditch.

The crew scrambled out from the Beaufort which sank in 90 seconds. By that time South African pilot Lieutenant E. T. Strever, Pilot Officer W. M. Dunsmore RAF and two New Zealand sergeants, A. R. Brown and J. A. Wilkinson had got themselves into the dinghy and had started paddling for the shore visible some four to five miles away. They made little progress until they realised they had not pulled in the sea anchor.

While they were paddling an Italian Air Force Cant 506 flying boat circled round, landed, and taxied to within a hundred yards of the dinghy. Lt Strever jumped overboard and swam to the Cant to test reception. To his surprise he was offered brandy and given a cigarette. He signalled for his crew to close in and all were received in the same way. The Cant then taxied round a headland and into Kérkyra harbour on the island of Corfu.

After landing the four prisoners were taken to a military camp where an Italian officer, who spoke good English, interpreted. Clothes were lent to them while their own were dried and all four were taken to the officers' mess and given a steak and tomato meal with wine. They were allowed the run of the mess, played cards and table tennis, and were *asked* not to run away! Given paper and envelopes, they were told that if they wished to inform their next-of-kin of their capture, the Italians would, provided the letters were left unsealed, pass them to the International Red Cross. Dinner was served at 20.00hrs with excellent food and wine and cigarettes in abundance. That night they were allotted officers' quarters, but there were sentries posted outside.

Next morning, although the Italians in the Continental fashion did not partake of breakfast, they rustled up some eggs for their prisoner guests. The Beaufort crew, uncertain of their future in a prisoner-of-war camp, made the best of the situation, ate well, and found it hard to refuse being photographed with Italian officers. To their surprise they discovered they were to be conveyed in to internment by aircraft—the same Cant flying boat—and in this they duly set course for Taranto across the Straits.

The Cant was crewed by a pilot, second pilot, engineer and wireless operator/observer, plus a corporal acting as armed escort. Suddenly Sgt Wilkinson, who had been awaiting an opportunity, smashed his fist under the observer's jaw and as he fell he dived over to the corporal, seized his revolver, and handed it to Lt Strever. The other two Beaufort crew members tackled the engineer. However, the second pilot glanced round at the disturbance, dropped into the forward well and grabbed a light automatic weapon. Sgt Wilkinson immediately followed up his actions by grabbing the unfortunate corporal and using him as a body shield to force his way forward to the second pilot whose gun was wrested from him. Meanwhile, the pilot lost height and appeared to be attempting a landing but Lt Strever jabbed the gun into his ribs and ordered him to level out. After the rest of the Beaufort crew had armed themselves with spanners and wrenches, the Italians were bound up one-by-one. The corporal appeared in a poor way and it transpired later that this was his first flight. He was violently airsick and so was propped up against an open port.

Lt Streven had taken over the controls, but without maps or charts or any knowledge of the speeds and fuel consumption, it was difficult to plan. The aircraft was still over the Straits, but eventually the toe of Italy came in sight and a rough course was worked out for Malta—fuel permitting. The second pilot was unbound and put in his seat to assist Lt Strever. He appeared to get very agitated as Malta was neared—this was a peak period in the Axis assault on the Island and the Spitfires of the defences were much feared. Not without good reason—three Spitfires suddenly attacked.

The Beaufort crew tried every way of identifying themselves. One Sergeant spun the guns to show that they had no intention of firing, the Pilot Officer took off his white vest and waved it outside, while the Lieutenant ordered the second pilot to land. As they landed, the engines stopped—the fuel had finally given out. The crew clambered out and waved; the Spitfires at last flew off and a motor launch came out to tow the flying boat in.

The crew were feeling some remorse at their rough handling of the Italians, particularly after the way they had been treated. An interpreter explained their regrets, but the Italians apparently took it well, one even insisting on opening and sharing a bottle of wine from his suitcase—taken because the crew were to have gone on leave after reaching Taranto!

Above right: A No 86 Squadron Beaufort operating from Malta over the Ionian Sea. / *IWM*

Right: Cant Z506B flying boat, captured by a Beaufort crew and flown to Malta, after which it was impressed into RAF service and given British national identity markings.

Torpedo and Train Mediterranean 1943

An unusual success came to one of No 39's Beauforts on January 14, 1943 as it patrolled ahead of a convoy some 136 miles south-east of Malta. The crew observed an Italian supply submarine and attacked it with depth charges. The bows were blown into the air by the explosion and the submarine stopped with a list to starboard. Crew members on deck were machine-gunned and signals were sent to naval units who soon came on the scene and finished the submarine off.

Between January 6 and 20, Beauforts in the Mediterranean area were out on 10 nights, dropping mines in Tunis and Sousse harbours, and in the same period made a similar number of anti-shipping patrols.

There was a grim determination to sink every enemy vessel located as it was realised that ability of the Axis to continue the fight in North Africa depended mainly on the supplies they received. The 9 955 ton German tanker *Thorsheimer* was spotted by a Baltimore on February 20 and ten Wellingtons and four Beauforts were detailed to attack it that night. Heavy electrical storms caused buffeting, drift, and interference on the ASV which was also being jammed by Axis ground stations. Only one Beaufort located the tanker and attacked. The tanker was not sunk but its crossing to Tunisia was delayed. The following night she was located again between Trapani and Cape Bon. Three Beauforts from No 39 Squadron on stand-by set out immediately from Malta and scored three hits with their three torpedoes, but still the tanker stayed afloat. An hour later a Beaufort delivered the fourth torpedo and hit the tanker again. It slowly settled down in the water and final reconnaissance at 02.00hrs next morning showed only a battered framework above water in the middle of a burning patch of oil.

At midday on March 17, nine Beauforts escorted by nine Beaufighters attacked a convoy in the Gulf of Taranto. Being close to the Italian mainland, the convoy had an umbrella of 15 Bf110s and Ju88s. These the Beaufighters held off while seven of the Beauforts managed to deliver torpedo attacks. One Beaufort and one Beaufighter were lost.

On shipping searches, ASV radar was used, known then for security reasons as the 'SI' (Special Installation). However, it was not so 'special' that the enemy did not know of it and attempt to reduce its efficiency by jamming the frequency from land stations on Sardinia and Sicily. As a counter-measure, operators could detune the receiver slightly which reduced the range of the equipment but allowed 'blips' to be seen through the clutter created by the jamming. By the end of February an anti-jamming circuit was fitted which, although it was not completely effective, did improve matters. From patrols at 500 feet a convoy of ships could be detected up to about 25 miles away.

As in the United Kingdom, so in the Middle East, Beaufighters took over from Beauforts during 1943 as the shipping strike force. Both No 39 Squadron and No 47 Squadron re-armed with Beaufighters at North African bases in June 1943, which meant that the Beaufort was no longer in RAF squadron service in the Middle East. A few were retained in SAAF squadron service for a short period, one of the last, DD898, being wrecked on July 6 when it swung on take-off and hit a Blenheim V, BA374.

The Beaufort remained for a time in a training role in the Middle East. Established in the Canal Zone to train torpedo-bomber crews was No 5 Middle East Torpedo School. Crews which had ferried out Beauforts from England after attending a course at a Torpedo Training Unit in Britain, were often sent to No 5 METS for re-training. Tactics and techniques were different. In the UK crews were taught how to make use of cloud over the approach but in the Mediterranean there were often cloudless skies for weeks. Similarly, UK trained crews had to learn to cope with the difficulties of height judgement over calm sunny seas. Beauforts and Wellingtons were the main types used for the School which was tasked additionally with training crews for Ceylon. Late in 1943 the school re-equipped with Beaufighters.

Beauforts had one last task in the Middle East. There was a shortage of qualified flying instructors for the various operational training units in the Near and Middle East. No personnel could be spared from the United Kingdom, so HQ Mediterranean Allied Air Forces decided to set up a training school from within their own resources. Accordingly, No 11 Flying Instructors School was formed in December 1943 in the Canal Zone initially equipped with nine Harvards and six Beauforts. However, in 1944, the Beauforts were replaced by Ansons.

Left: Significant to success in the Mediterranean was the ASV repeater screen seen on the right of the pilot's cockpit. The long rubber visor is to permit him to see the cathode ray tube in daylight. / *IWM*

Above: A 'yagi' aerial of the ASV beneath the fuselage. The central streamlined projection is the pitot head of the air speed indicator. / *IWM*

Below: Beaufort I of a training unit in the Middle East.

Beware Your Friends

It is a fact that, in spite of all the mine-laying, bombing and torpedo-bombing, that Beauforts carried out throughout the war, more were lost through accident than enemy action. Operations were sporadic, but training went on all the time and took a steady toll of crews and aircraft.

Most distressing of all was accidental destruction by friendly aircraft through mis-identification. Fortunately the Beaufort did not suffer as much in this way as the Blenheim or Beaufighter. There were, however, two very tragic errors. Beaufort L9809 of No 3 OTU Chivenor was shot down in mistake for a Ju88 by a Hurricane of No 504 Squadron operating from Exeter on the night of June 16/17, 1941. Only one of the four crew members escaped. The other mistake was in full daylight. A Beaufort from No 100 Squadron, Royal Australian Air Force, on July 12, 1942 was on a sea search over St George's Channel (separating New Britain from New Ireland) when a Liberator crew, passing over, mistook it for a Japanese aircraft and shot it down. Realising too late their tragic mistake, they circled low over the water and dropped a raft, food and flares to the crew seen struggling in the water. Unfortunately, in spite of 250 flying hours being spent by searching aircraft, the Beaufort's crew was never found.

Defences both active and passive damaged Beaufort L4479 of No 3 Operational Training Unit on February 4, 1941. The pilot left Silloth at dusk to fly to Squires Gate and found that he was unable to switch on his wingtip navigation lights. The Merseyside defences, having good reason to be jumpy, presumed the Beaufort to be a Ju88 and opened up, hitting one engine. Immediately the aircraft started losing height. Seeing the coastline at Morecambe below, the pilot skilfully brought the Beaufort to a landing on the sands. Unfortunately a concrete obstruction post, placed to prevent an enemy landing, was in the path of the landing run. The aircraft was damaged and one of the crew injured.

Things went very wrong for a crew of No 217 Squadron Beaufort in the late afternoon of January 1942. They checked their position on return from a patrol flight and for some unexplained reason received a wrong vector from a direction finding station which brought them over the Dover balloon barrage. When flying at around 160 knots at 2 800 feet in the darkening sky, a wing of their Beaufort slammed into the cable of a balloon flying at 4 000 feet. The impact slewed the Beaufort completely round and the cable, which parted 500 feet above and 800 feet below the aircraft, being suddenly released of its tension, looped over the wing. This caused the Beaufort to go into a spin. By almost superhuman efforts the pilot regained control a mere 400 feet over Dover, and immediately headed out to sea to jettison the bombs. A fire started in the starboard engine but this was quickly put out by the automatic extinguishers. Unbeknown to the crew the cable hanging over the wing damaged the underbelly of the aircraft as it whipped in the slipstream. This caused a parachute stowed in the crew compartment to billow out and slow the Beaufort almost to stalling speed, making it extremely difficult to control. Cautiously heading his jerking aircraft back to the coast, which was crossed at Ramsgate, the pilot was unaware of the consternation he was causing on the ground.

It was not only the roar of the Taurus engines at full throttle reverberating in the streets that shook the inhabitants of Ramsgate. There was also the sudden shattering of a lamp-post and a shower of slates from the roofs of houses. The pilot, nursing his Beaufort, realised he was inordinately low but not only was he unaware of the trailing cable he was also ignorant of the fact its whipping of the fuselage had so damaged the bomb doors, that they had stuck. The bombs he thought were safely deposited in the Channel were rolling loose in the bomb-bay. It was as well that the crew were unaware of this final twist of fate for they may well have been tempted to fly on and struggle for height in order to bale out. As it was they landed safely on the emergency runway at Manston. When the aircraft was examined the next morning, the 1 300 feet of cable was still looped round the wing with its ends hanging. It had cut cleanly into the wing to a depth of 18 inches.

The crew of W6495, returning tired from patrol with an unserviceable radio and short of fuel on March 18, 1942, were misled by friendly defences in a strange way. To protect their North African base, a dummy airfield had been erected in the empty desert nearby and equipped with landing lights to attract enemy bombers. It had, in fact, become a directional guide to aircraft returning to the main base, and the absence of its light on this night led the crew to believe that they were still over enemy territory. Forced to land in the dark through lack of fuel, they struck a ridge on the run-in, causing the aircraft to finish up on its back, severely jolting the crew and injuring one of them.

The chief danger from friendly aircraft was the risk of collision when flying in formation, particularly during turns. On May 11, 1942, two Beauforts of a No 42 Squadron formation collided in a formation turn—AW366 broke in two and plunged into the sea, but AW310 managed a safe landing at Leuchars. And not only aircraft of the same formation were involved. As a result of a Malta-based Baltimore sighting two merchant vessels, escorted by four destroyers north-east of Benghazi in the afternoon of October 25, 1942, No 47 Squadron's Beauforts at Shandur were made ready. A strike was planned the following day when further surveillance suggested that the ships would be some 20 miles off Tobruk. Bisleys of No 15 (SAAF) Squadron were to make a bombing atack, co-ordinated with a Beaufort torpedo attack. The Bisleys went in so low that one hit a merchant man's mast, pulled away and then crashed. The Beauforts followed up so quickly that one ship was hit almost simultaneously by a bomb and a torpedo and Beaufort DE110 and a Bisley swung into each other and both crashed into the sea.

Fortunately there is no record of Beauforts being brought down by friendly fire from the ground but three nearly were. The crew of a trawler off the British coast on November 21, 1941, were convinced that Beaufort AW192 of No 86 Squadron, flying low over the water, was a German aircraft. They opened up with their machine-gun and cursed because it apparently had no effect. But when the Beaufort landed it slewed off the runway—a tyre had

BEAUFORT II
TWIN WASP S3C4-G
8/41

Above: The ground crew had their hazards too. Even this hardstanding at Filton is a little waterlogged, but at Leuchars on one occasion a maintenance crew had to row out to a Beaufort to service it! / *Bristol Aeroplane Company*

Right: View from the turret of a Beaufort of a following flight. Precision formations were not practised because of the dangers of collision, but a closed-in formation was desirable to concentrate defensive fire if attacked. / *IWM*

been punctured by a bullet. When Beaufort JM454 landed at Kemble after a test flight at the Overseas Aircraft Despatch Unit on November 17, 1943 there were some jagged holes in her. The cause was presumed to be anti-aircraft fire from ships in the British Channel. Next month from the same unit, LS143 was damaged by shrapnel over land. This time the cause was flying too near a gunnery range.

There were more dangers to flying Beauforts than the enemy.

British-built Beauforts in other Forces

Beauforts of the South African Air Force 1941-43

In late 1941 Beauforts were sent to the South African Air Force who wished to have a torpedo-bomber available in case a German commerce raider approached the Cape and its strategic sea routes. After Japan's entry into the war, South African coastal defence became even more imperative and some Beauforts were transferred to the South African Air Force from those flying to the Middle East. Nos 36 and 37 Coastal Defence Flights had been formed with Ansons early in 1942 and the first was re-equipped with Beauforts and the other partly re-equipped. After a third Coastal Flight equipped with Marylands was formed, the three flights were amalgamated into No 20 (SAAF) Squadron and flew up to East Africa for Operation Ironclad, the occupation of Madagascar.

Because of the strategic importance of Madagascar (now the Malagasy Republic) and fears that the Japanese might use this Vichy-controlled island as a base for submarines, the British Government decided to occupy it, taking first the harbour area of Diego Suarez.

The expeditionary force of three brigades had as its air support the Fleet Air Arm squadrons on the carriers HMS *Indomitable* and HMS *Illustrious,* plus units of the South African Air Force. Landings were made successfully on May 5, 1942 and two days later resistance in the area ceased. To assist in the next stage, the capture of the whole of the island, the six Marylands and 16 Beauforts of No 20 Squadron flew into Arrachart airfield near Diego Suarez on May 12. They had come from the Union and staged via Lindi on the Tanganyikan coast, accompanied by 12 Lodestars carrying ground personnel and equipment.

A four months lull followed before operations were continued to occupy the vast bulk of the island. The delay was partly due to the diversion of supporting forces to the Middle East. During this time No 20 Squadron carried out reconnaissance work for the land and naval forces. In the course of the patrols two unidentified submarines were reported. The squadron had considerable difficulty, however, in keeping the Beauforts serviceable. Spares for only one month's flying had been flown in, and there were difficulties in obtaining others as the Beaufort was not a SAAF standard aircraft type. On September 4 the Squadron was re-numbered No 16 Squadron SAAF, and transferred from the operational control of SAAF headquarters in Pretoria to No 207 Group (East Africa) responsible to HQ RAF Middle East; this helped to improve the supply of spares.

Operations were resumed on September 20. To stop the Vichy authorities withdrawing rolling stock southward on the railway, the air component supporting the land forces was ordered to destroy a large concrete bridge spanning a ravine on the Betsiboka river. A Maryland, three Albacores and three Beauforts tried without success to achieve this on three successive days; then the situation

G. 1437
F. A/C ON TARMAC
. BAY B.C. 20-1-42

changed as the land forces by-passed this stretch of railway.

Gradually the land forces worked their way southward. It was thought that the few remaining Vichy French aircraft were using Ihosy airfield in the south of the island as a base. On October 8, three Beaufort crews, circling the airfield prior to bombing, noticed some aircraft hidden in bushes a mile or so away. These they raked with fire and then photographed—revealing three Potez 253s, a Potez 63 and a Morane 406. A number of attacks were then made on these aircraft and the hangar at Ihosy. The latter had 59 bombs aimed at it before a direct hit was scored damaging beyond repair the two military and two civilian aircraft inside. Subsequently two Goeland passenger aircraft were found hidden in the bush.

In this campaign, Beauforts forming 'B' flight of No 16 Squadron, made 34 operational sorties and lost four aircraft through crash-landings, attributable in the main to engine failure. In November the Beaufort crews started to convert to Blenheims.

Beauforts of the Royal Canadian Air Force 1941-47

Canada requested a batch of Beauforts early in 1941 and 12 Mk Is were shipped out in the late summer. On December 9 that year Canada declared war on Japan following the Japanese attacks on Pearl Harbour and landings in Malaya. It was conceivable that Japanese

Above: The Beaufort in South African service. A Beaufort I of No 16 Squadron, SAAF. / *South African Air Force*

Left: Line-up at No 32 Operational Training Unit, Patricia Bay, British Columbia, on January 20, 1942; left to right, three Beaufort Is and three Ansons. The two Beauforts nearest the camera, N1006 and L9967, are coded RD.B and RD.K respectively. / *Public Archives of Canada*

Below: Beaufort I of No 149 (TB) Squadron, Royal Canadian Air Force, on patrol over Patricia Bay, British Columbia, June 18, 1943. This aircraft became instructional airframe A375 when its flying days finished early in 1944. / *Public Archives of Canada*

surface ships could menace the west coast of Canada and the Beauforts were first used by No 149 RCAF torpedo-bomber squadron and No 32 Operational Training Unit at Patricia Bay in British Columbia. As it was, they were not needed in a strike role and mainly did patrol work. Five were involved in mishaps and withdrawn from service and all were taken off flying duties in 1944. Nine were used as instructional airframes of which the last A383 (ex-N1027) was finally discarded by the RCAF in March 1947.

Beauforts of the Turkish Air Force 1944-47

A treaty of alliance with Turkey was signed by Great Britain and France at Ankara on October 19, 1939 but after the German successes in the early war years, which brought German forces to Turkey's borders, the Turks signed a treaty of friendship with Germany. Both the Allies and the Axis supplied Turkey with aircraft and Beauforts were among British aircraft types supplied from August 2, 1944 when Turkey broke off diplomatic relations with Germany. The Beauforts were flown to Turkey via Habbaniya in Iraq from surpluses held in the Middle East in 1944; early in 1945 additional trainer versions were supplied. Later Beaufighters were supplied and only the trainer versions of the Beaufort were widely used in Turkish service. After extensive American military aid in 1947, the British aircraft were discarded.

Streamline and Scrap

Ironically, once the Beaufort had left squadron service in the United Kingdom, production more than met requirements. Further orders were placed, but to avoid holding up the production of Beaufighters at Filton, Beaufort production there was halted. The last 250 were assembled at the new Banwell factory from components built by sub-contractors.

From mid-1943 onwards the Beaufort became almost exclusively a trainer, nevertheless an operational trainer. Coastal Command operational training was a lengthy process since, after flying training, pilots and observers had to be proficient in maritime reconnaissance (then termed general reconnaissance) and additionally skilled in torpedo dropping and torpedo attack techniques. The Torpedo Training Unit, established as a separate unit, had been incorporated in No 5 Operational Training Unit in 1942, but in 1943 with Beauforts available in numbers, the training organisation of Coastal Command expanded.

From the operations related earlier, it will be seen that there were many occasions when Beaufort strikes were made with little result. This evoked some criticism from naval circles to the effect that the RAF lacked an appreciation of the importance of torpedo-bombing and that crews were not properly trained for this work. The criticism was probably a little unfair, as the RAF at the time had their hands full in many directions; perhaps the very emphasis on the build-up of Bomber Command, and the growing strength of Fighter Command, made the torpedo-bombing element of Coastal Command appear a quite insignificant part of the Royal Air Force.

Action was soon taken by the RAF. A Torpedo Refresher School had been formed on the last day of 1942 at Leuchars, but something much more comprehensive was needed. On January 11, 1943, No 1 Torpedo Training Unit was formed with Beauforts, followed by No 2, each with a Group Captain in command, which gave them both RAF station status. The units were each initially tasked with training 76 crews for overseas, Nos 1 & 2 specialising on day and night attacks respectively. It was estimated that 300 practice torpedo drops were necessary before a crew could be deemed proficient.

As it was, the efforts of the TTUs were rather a waste of time. Because of the lack of communication between overseas and home commands, Beaufort crews continued to be trained although the type was no longer in operational use, and re-training on Beaufighters and other types had become necessary.

During 1943 Beauforts were being widely used in operational training units and were essential at the conversion stage although crews would be going on to Beaufighters. The new Beaufighter strike aircraft, armed with rockets and the 'Torbeau' torpedo-carrying version had only half the crew of a Beaufort. These two crew

A number of late-serving Beaufort Is and IIs were given the white Coastal Command finish in their role of ASV training. Photo taken September 27, 1943. / *IWM*

members were in tandem, and as there was no room for side-by-side seating the pilot sat alone in the cockpit. It was too much of a step to expect trainee pilots to go straight from the Ansons or Oxfords of the flying training schools to operational training on Beaufighters without dual instruction and the Beaufort was used as an intermediate step for this purpose.

At OTUs the proportion of Beauforts was usually half the main operational type. In mid-1943 No 2 OTU at Catfoss had an establishment for 30 Beaufighters to 15 Beauforts, plus two Ansons and four target tug aircraft. No 9 OTU at Crosby-on-Eden and No 132 OTU at East Fortune had similar numbers. The trend was to increase the number of Beaufighters and reduce on Beauforts, but retaining sufficient to effect pilot conversion.

It was not only in Coastal Command that Beauforts were required as trainers. Beaufighters were used as night fighters by Fighter Command who operated some Beauforts with Beaufighters in No 54 OTU at Charter Hall in Scotland.

Many of the older Beaufort Is that had not been shipped overseas were ending their days in operational training units. Richard Gentil in his account of RAF wartime training 'Trained to Intrude' (Bachman & Turner 1974) wrote 'It was necessary to give us the feel of a powerful machine by an intermediate stage on an aircraft permitting an instructor to be at the pilot's side. The nearest approach was the Beaufort, which we would fly dual for a few hours. I was extremely glad to see the end of this experience. The machine vibrated at every seam, and wallowed in the air, but we satisfied everybody that we could fly even this, if necessary.'

No 5 OTU continued to be the main operator of Beauforts and more were lost from this unit than from any other. Some accidents are still unresolved, such as that to DD871 which set off on a war experience flight on

December 2, 1942 and of which nothing has been heard since. Mystery still surrounds the recovery of N1003 which force-landed on a navigational exercise in County Donegal, Eire. Provided the German Embassy were not aware of such incidents, it was possible to arrange a clandestine deal with the Irish authorities for a plain clothes party of pilot and ground crew to effect entry to Eire to carry out repairs and fly the aircraft back. Sometimes a Lysander was flown in with a pilot and mechanic for this purpose. The essence of such operations was swiftness and secrecy. The possibility of No 5 OTU's Beauforts violating Irish neutrality increased from early 1943 when the unit, having moved from Chivenor to Turnberry, moved on to Long Kesh in Northern Ireland (now the Maze prison) to make room for one of the new torpedo training units at Turnberry.

At Long Kesh the very nature of torpedo-bomber operational training led to a number of accidents through the incidental low flying. The American pilot of DX134, Sgt R. K. Holmes, was killed in this way. Flying low over Church Island near Bellaghy in County Londonderry, he failed to allow for the church steeple on the island and in banking steeply to avoid it, stalled in from 100 feet.

Beauforts had been sent to the Far East to meet a threat that did not develop. No 22, the first Beaufort squadron, after intensive flying on operations in Britain up to February 1942, started moving to the Far East the following month, staging through Malta and flying a few operations from the island in the process. They were scheduled to re-deploy to a base in Ceylon in April 1942, to defend the island from the Japanese fleet—at the very month the Japanese carriers threatened the island and air attacks were made on the naval base of Trincomalee and Colombo harbour.

Blenheims of No 11 Squadron were the only RAF aircraft in Ceylon capable of bombing missions against the

Japanese fleet and although they made an attempt, their attacks were ineffective. The Beauforts in taking over 100 days *en route*, arrived too late and lost the opportunity of striking at the Japanese fleet; a successful foray on their part at this time could have altered the course of the Pacific War. As it was, they were held in readiness at Ratmalana, near Colombo, against any further threat which, in the event, never came. The squadron was joined by No 217 Squadron also from the United Kingdom, which had similarly been delayed for operations in the Mediterranean. Their personnel arrived in July 1942 and received Hudsons as interim equipment until April 1943 when a few Beauforts arrived. In July, however, they were once again a fully-equipped Beaufort squadron.

The two squadrons in Ceylon used the airfields of Trincomalee in the east and Ratmalana in the west; at the latter No 3 Torpedo Refresher School was established, equipped with Beauforts. Although there were no operations, apart from operational patrols and regular radar calibration flights, there was the inevitable wastage of Beauforts, both *en route* and after arrival; DW826 and DW832 were both lost in flying accidents in Ceylon. Both squadrons were re-equipped with Beaufighters in June 1944.

One other Beaufort squadron served for a short period in the Far East. This was No 42 which, after withdrawal from operations in the United Kingdom, re-assembled in India with Beauforts for coastal patrol in case of a Japanese assault. But with this possibility receding, the squadron was equipped with Blenheim Vs and moved to Burma.

There had been throughout the war an eastward shift of Beaufort concentration from the United Kingdom to the Middle East and then to the Far East. Further east still, in Australasia, the Beaufort concentration was also growing.

The final Beauforts built in Britain were to a new standard, purely as trainers, known as the Beaufort Mk II(T). These aircraft, delivered from August 1943 to November 25, 1944 when the last Beaufort left the factory, had no rear turret; instead the position was faired over giving the aircraft a streamlined appearance. The Royal Navy, which earlier had acquired the Mk Is for use in the Mediterranean, were particularly interested in the new trainer version and acquired 38 from the RAF.

During 1945 the trainer version of the Beauforts replaced the earlier versions in training units. The Beaufort I was withdrawn in 1944 and the Mk II in July 1945 with the proviso that the Twin Wasp engines were to be salvaged. The Mk II(T) was withdrawn from service just under a year later.

At the beginning of 1946, the total holding of Beauforts in RAF store was a single Mk I, 13 Mk IIs, 49 Mk II(T)s of which 43 were being prepared for long term storage and 42 additionally tropicalised for service overseas. The single Mk I was held as part of a policy, instituted by the Air Ministry after both World Wars, to keep an example of RAF aircraft types used in numbers, However, storage presented problems and the number of aircraft to be preserved was drastically pruned. During 1946 and 1947 several hundred of the remaining Beaufort airframes were 'reduced to produce' at the giant plants at Cowley and Eaglescliffe.

Built and Blooded in the Antipodes. The first six Australian ~ built

Singapore in the 'thirties was seen as Britain's bastion in the East. It had been a major port of call on the shipping route to Australia for a hundred years and was becoming a vital staging post in the newly established air route to Australia. Since any challenge to Singapore's security was only likely to be from a naval power, the defence of the island against attack relied mostly upon coastal guns and two squadrons of Vickers Vildebeest biplane torpedo-bombers. When the Australian Government invited a British Air Mission to discuss regional defence, with a view towards developing the Commonwealth's aircraft industry, it was mutually agreed that defence needs would best be met by producing a GR aircraft. Australia had a vast coastline to defend, and it was probable that Britain would need to place orders to replace, or reinforce, the ageing Vildebeests at Singapore. Undoubtedly, the new Bristol Beaufort was the aircraft to build. The very name was right—for to the antipodes Beaufort was not an English ducal estate, but a town in North Borneo, halfway between Australia and Singapore.

On July 1, 1939, an order for 180 Beaufort airframes and adequate spares was placed with the newly-formed Beaufort Division of the Commonwealth's Department of Aircraft Production, to be produced at the Commonwealth Aircraft Corporation factory, Fisherman's Bend, Melbourne, Victoria. To expedite production, drawings, jigs and tools were supplied by the Bristol Aeroplane Company while new buildings were erected including an assembly plant at Mascot, New South Wales.

The Taurus engines and airframe components with involved production techniques were shipped from England, together with complete parts for an initial six aircraft. Work was speeded up when war came and in October 1939 the eighth British production Beaufort (L4448) was shipped out to Australia as a sample aircraft.

The call on Allied shipping, and the sinking of merchantmen by Axis submarines, seriously disrupted production and then, in May 1940, Britain placed an embargo on the export of war materials due to the desperate situation evolving in Europe. To build the Taurus in Australia would mean long delays in tooling up, so it was proposed to change the power unit to the American 1 200hp Pratt & Whitney Wasp, already installed in the Lockheed Hudsons being delivered to the Royal Australian Air Force from America.

After using the pattern aircraft L4448 for trials with the new engines in the spring of 1941, an initial order for Wasps was placed in America and a factory set up at Lidcombe, NSW, to ensure a supply within the

Commonwealth. Simultaneously, at the Bristol works at Filton, Beaufort N1110 was fitted with Wasps to test the installation for design stress and aerodynamic aspects. The British Ministry of Aircraft Production welcomed a change to a standard American engine. It gave the opportunity of closing down production of the special-to-type Taurus engine and permitted an increase in Hercules engine output, needed for the four-engined Halifax bomber and not least for the Beaufighter which was to succeed the Beaufort. Thus, in Britain the Wasp-engined version went into production as the Beaufort Mk II and, allowing Mks III to IV for further development of British-built versions, the initial Australian Wasp-powered Beauforts were designated Mk V.

During these delays in finalising the design of the Australian Beaufort, large-scale production was planned with railway workshops playing a major part as area workshops using local industries. Shops at Chullora,

Above: Pattern for production. L4448, the eighth production Beaufort airframe in Britain seen being rolled out after re-assembly in Australia as pattern aircraft for Beaufort production there using Pratt & Whitney Twin Wasp engines. It made its first flight in Australia during May 1941 at Mascot, NSW. / *Australian War Memorial*

Right: The first Beaufort in Australia. The Filton-built L4448 on flying trials. / *Australian War Memorial*

Above: A forlorn hope. The first Beauforts off the Australian production lines were sent to Singapore – and returned to Australia as they could not be used effectively. They are seen here being refuelled by an RAF tanker. / *IWM*

Above right: Cheerful optimism in Singapore in December 1941, but within weeks the Beauforts were withdrawn and Singapore had fallen. / *IWM*

Right: The Beaufort Vs from Australia, viewed speculatively at Singapore. / *IWM*

NSW, were made responsible for front fuselage, under-carriage, stern frames and nacelles; Newport, Victoria, for rear fuselage and empennage, and Islington, South Australia, for mainplanes including the centre-section.

The first Australian-assembled Beaufort flew from Fisherman's Bend to RAAF Station Laverton on May 5, 1941, but the first fully Australian-built example was not completed until the following August. Because of Britain's plight it was decided that the initial Beauforts could be offset against an order the RAF had placed for 100 Australian-built models. This was partly reciprocal, since Britain had offset to Australia some of her Lend/Lease aircraft from America. Further, when the embargo on exports was lifted on the Lend/Lease Act becoming effective, Britain promised Australia 50 of the new Beaufighters from December 1941.

It was a fateful December. The Japanese struck Pearl Harbour on the 7th. Only a week later they were advancing on Singapore through Malaya and had attacked Borneo lying between Singapore and Australia in their seven-pronged assault. The Commonwealth itself was in danger, particularly the sparsely populated tropical Northern Territories. At this time the maritime reconnaissance role at Singapore and in Australia, fell to the 50-odd Lockheed Hudsons in service with the RAAF.

Among the 250 British and Commonwealth first-line aircraft in South-East Asia there was a single Australian-built Beaufort available for operations. It was stationed at Kota Bharu in Malaya as a special reconnaissance aircraft under the direct control of Air Headquarters, Singapore.

When its crew were ordered to reconnoitre north of Singora (Songkla), to find out if Japanese landings had taken place in Thailand, theirs was the first operational sortie by an Australian-built aircraft. This Beaufort, riddled with bullet holes from Japanese fighter attacks, brought back irrefutable evidence of Japanese presence. The Beaufort was written off, so badly was it damaged, but the crew were unscathed. They reported Japanese ships landing troops on the Singora-Patani seafront and photos taken by them, and rushed to Singapore by a Brewster Buffalo, showed 60 Japanese aircraft on Singora airfield.

There were no other Beauforts available. Only six had so far been completed and though they had been sent immediately to Singapore where, not properly armed and with untrained crews using a type new to that sphere, they were more of a liability than an asset. Except for the single aircraft retained for photo reconnaissance by Air Head-quarters, the rest were returned. It was not an auspicious operational debut for the Beaufort in the Far East.

Commonwealth Confrontation. Australasia 1942

In January 1942 the Japanese invaded the Netherland East Indies, Celebes and North Borneo, and landed at Rabaul in New Britain and Lae in New Guinea. The following month Singapore fell and an attack was made on Australian territory at Darwin. The next operational Beaufort sorties were in defence of Australia itself.

A daring reconnaissance by a Japanese submarine-borne floatplane over Sydney harbour on May 31, preceded a midget submarine attack on the harbour that night, and was followed by a spate of merchant ship sinkings in the area over the next few weeks. Beauforts, stationed at Richmond, joined Hudsons in patrolling the seaboard from early June.

At Richmond, on February 25, the first Australian Beaufort squadron had formed. Its designation, No 100 Squadron, represented a considerable jump in the sequence of Royal Australian Air Force squadron allocations and was adopted in honour of No 100 Squadron RAF, whose Vildebeest torpedo-bombers had fought so valiantly at Singapore. When the squadron moved northward to Cairns in May, as part of its working-up period, training had continued at Richmond.

Operating Australia's first bomber, the squadron's training was more rigidly supervised than most; in spite of the desperate situation, it was edged carefully into operations. At Mareeba, sharing the airfield with American and Australian units, the squadron started patrolling Queensland's coastline. Then came detached flights northward across the Great Barrier Reef to Port Moresby on the southern side of New Guinea to acclimatise the crews to equatorial conditions.

When a Japanese ship was reported making in the direction of Lae on the other side of New Guinea, the Beauforts of No 100 Squadron were ordered to strike. Wing Commander J. R. Balmer led a flight of five from Mareeba to Moresby on June 25. While two Beauforts already at Moresby on crew orientation set off on a diversionary raid to Salamaua, Balmer led the shipping strike that night, the four other Beauforts following at 20-minute intervals.

From the latest intelligence reports suggesting the ships must be nearing Lae and that sounds of the slightly earlier diversionary raids would cause the ships to turn eastward to avoid detction by returning bombers in the bright moonlight, Balmer accurately forecast the enemy's position. Following the training pattern, he lined up his target along the moonpath and moved in at a mere 50 feet—only to have his bombs fail to release. A second attack had the same frustrating result. On a third run, in spite of intense anti-aircraft fire, he pulled the jettison lever to drop all the bombs at once; his gunner reported two hits.

Two of the following Beauforts made low runs and scored hits; one was badly damaged by anti-aircraft fire and made a wheels-up landing at Moresby. The other two had attacked the port of Lae. However, of the two on the diversionary raid, one failed to return; the first Australian Beaufort had been lost on operations. It was last heard at some 60 miles distant, after raiding the Salamaua Isthmus, requesting a bearing. No other message was received and Sqn Ldr C. W. L. Sage and his crew in A9-52 were reported missing.

At this time the Beaufighter, supplied from England, was coming into use and plans were being made to produce it in Australia. In the UK the strike role of the Beaufort squadrons had already been taken over by Beaufighter squadrons, but in the Far East at this time the Beaufighter was regarded as a long-range fighter. In any case it would take time to tool up for Beaufighters, meanwhile more Beauforts were needed and production continued. This was before the Torbeau had been introduced and the Beaufort was the only aircraft equipped for torpedo-attacks. A special mobile torpedo unit was formed to follow No 100 into the field, in case opportunities should arise to attack the Japanese fleet. The Australians had learnt a lesson from reports of the Channel fiasco in the English Channel earlier that year.

The chance for torpedo attack came. The squadron had gone south to Laverton, and again a detachment went northwards to New Guinea for operations when units of the Japanese fleet were sighted in the Solomon Sea. This time Wg Cdr Balmer led five of No 100 Squadron's Beauforts to a strip at Milne Bay on the eastern tip of the island where RAAF Kittyhawks were stationed. They were joined by three Beaufighters from No 30 Squadron, the first Australian unit to fly this aircraft. On September 7, a Hudson crew sighted an enemy cruiser and destroyer within striking distance and the Australian Beauforts' first torpedo attack was mounted that afternoon. The three Beaufighters took-off, one of them crashing in the process, to divert the warship fire. Hudsons, escorted by Kittyhawks, went in to bomb the ships to add to their confusion, while the Beauforts carefully made their torpedo runs—and missed! The warships then entered Milne Bay and shelled the shoreline, but it was the last time they did. The Australians, with American assistance, were establishing a halt line to the Japanese invasion well to the north of their homeland.

A night torpedo attack in the early hours of October 4 was equally ineffective. Wg Cdr Balmer led ten Beauforts on a shipping strike off the Shortland Islands over 400 miles distant. Squalls as they neared their target blotted out the moonlight and some crews lost touch with the main formation. Seven crews sighted ships and made torpedo drops, but no hits were seen. One Beaufort failed to return. An enquiry was made into the failure and again

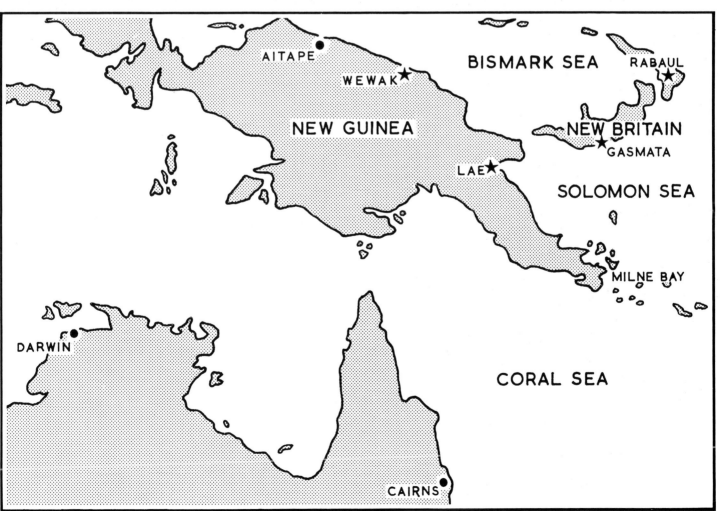

the squadron was withdrawn for further training, but the crews protested that it was the torpedoes that were defective.

Soon back on operations, the squadron was detailed for an attack on enemy destroyers on the night of November 24. Ten aircraft were loaded up at their dispersal pens, six with torpedoes and four with 500 and 250lb bombs. As one of the engines of a torpedo-armed aircraft was started up it burst into flames. The armament officer, Plt Off R. A. J. Duncan, and helpers rushed to the aircraft and at great personal risk moved the torpedo from its rack. In the target area there was poor weather and again four crews failed to find their targets, but the pilot of A9-42 claimed a hit on the stern of a Japanese destroyer with a 500-pounder. Again, a Beaufort was lost but, fortunately, not the crew. Sergeant J. R. Duncan managed to ditch A9-2 on the shores of Collingwood Bay, from where his injured crew managed to link up with Australian troops.

In between strikes, much routine patrolling and searching was carried out by the Beauforts in an effort to gauge Japanese intentions. Early on December 2, Sgt C. R. Green's crew in A9-38 spotted four destroyers approaching Buna and signalled Base Operations at Milne Bay for instructions. The reply was brief and unequivocal—'shadow to limit of endurance and attack'. Sergeant Green estimated that fuel would allow two hours of shadowing, and he circled the destroyers at maximum visual range. When the time was up, and he was positioning for an attack, three Zeros came on to the scene and evasive action had to be taken immediately. Diving, twisting and turning the Beaufort shook off the fighters, the gunner claiming one 'probable' and one 'damaged'. That night another Beaufort strike was planned. This time a Hudson set out with the six Beauforts to drop flares to illuminate the target. Three torpedo drops were made and a resulting explosion suggested a hit, but this could not be confirmed.

Practice torpedo runs continued to be made by the squadron and these too, exacted a toll. The pilot of A9-29 on December 22, evidently misjudging a practice run-in, crashed into the waters of Milne Bay.

Throughout 1942, Lockheed Hudsons had been bearing the brunt of the patrolling and bombing but Bostons and Mitchel¹ squadrons were arriving in the theatre. Of the 30 squadrons the Royal Australian Air Force had in the field at the end of 1942 only one was of Beauforts. Plans early in 1943 were for force strength to be raised to 45 squadrons as soon as possible and to 51 by the end of that year with six Beaufort squadrons. To help protect the Australian homeland, two Hudson squadrons were receiving Beauforts to assist in daily reconnaissance patrols, No 7 Squadron at Ross River, Queensland, and No 14 Squadron at Pearce, Western Australia. But the main theatre of operations was to be in the various islands to the north, where Japanese incursions into Australasia had stopped short of the Commonwealth itself. The task was now a hard long slogging match to oust the Japanese and push them steadily back. In this the Beauforts had a major support task.

The three main means of attack of Australian Beauforts . . .

. . . *Above left:* by bombs, seen dropping from the open bomb bay of Mk VIII A9-427, 'Superman' of No 100 Squadron which did a record 145 sorties . . .

. . . *Below left:* by torpedo carried recessed under the fuselage seen just after the moment of release . . .

. . . *Below:* or by strafing with guns seen on this Mk VIII of No 100 Squadron mounted in the nose and turret. / *Australian War Memorial*

Beaufort Build-up. Australasia 1943

In the New Year, January 6, 1943 the Beaufort crews of the RAAF achieved the success that they had striven for so gallantly, but it was at a cost. No 100 Squadron launched six of their aircraft in a night torpedo attack on a convoy approaching Gasmata. Two transports were sunk and a light cruiser was damaged, but low-lying cloud shrouded the Port Moresby landing strip when they returned in darkness. Beaufort A9-8 crashed into a mountain near the airstrip and the wreckage of A9-32 was discovered later on Normanby Island.

When an opportunity to strike was next presented, the squadron's efforts were frustrated. Eight Beauforts, all armed with torpedoes, took off from Milne Bay two hours before dawn on March 3 to seek the reported targets. Thick cloud obscured the sea most of the way, so that only two crews spotted the enemy; of these one had a torpedo hang-up and the other dropped and missed.

To back up No 100 Squadron and other Beaufort units forming up in Australia, No 1 Operational Training Unit, East Sale, was using some Beauforts for crew training, but had suffered losses, including a number over the sea. Since this was an Australian-built aircraft and the other aircraft used were American or British, ugly rumours circulated that rough Australian workmanship was responsible. A judicial enquiry was ordered and its findings were that the losses could not be attributed to any one source. Later a Beaufort (A9-171) was to complete over 1 000 flying hours at No 1 OTU.

Certainly the Beaufort, workhorse though it was to become, was initially a disappointment to the RAAF. While production had improved and by May 8, 1943, 303 had been delivered, 51 of these had been lost and some 130 were temporarily unserviceable. The average unserviceability of Beaufort units was 52% of unit establishment, higher than any other aircraft type in Australian service. This was partly due to production difficulties which caused five different versions to be used.

The first 50 Beauforts from the line, Mk Vs, had Pratt & Whitney Twin Wasp S3C4-G engines locally-built by General Motors-Holden Ltd and fitted with Curtiss electric propellers. When the supply of these was threatened, American-built S1C3-G were obtained to engine the next 100. These engines were very similar except that they had single-speed blowers instead of two-speed blowers of the Australian licence-built version. But there were Curtiss airscrews for only 40, which became the Beaufort VI. The following 60 as Beaufort VII had Hamilton Standard propellers. By that time local production had picked up and a further 30 aircraft (the 151st to 180th) had the local-built S3C4-G with Hamilton Standard airscrews.

Additional orders had been placed to raise production from the initial 180 to 700. It was decided to maintain a new standard using Australian-built engines and incorporate various improvements. This new version, the Mk VIII, would be able to carry American as well as Australian torpedoes, had gimbal-mounted nose guns instead of fixed wing guns, a Blenheim-type Bristol Mk V turret with twin Browning guns and the British ASV. It would incorporate all the detailed modifications to date, including a new fin of increased area incorporated on the 91st-built and retrospectively included on some built earlier. The first Beaufort VIII left the lines in November 1942. In the spring of 1943 there were sufficient to supply Mk VIIIs first to the operational No 100 Squadron and then for Nos 6 and 8 Squadrons, to gain experience with the type prior to operations. The earlier versions were relegated to training units.

Meanwhile, No 100 continued as the only operational Beaufort squadron. To attack targets in New Britain, Goodenough Island was used to provide two airfields, one for fighters and another for bombers. Goodenough was mountainous island and sites were difficult to find, but RAAF Works Squadrons cleared a patch of forest at Vivigani to make a temporary field. The first aircraft to land there were six Beauforts of No 100 Squadron from Gurney airfield at Milne Bay who arrived during the afternoon of May 17, 1943. That same night they operated against Gasmata.

A clash with the dreaded Japanese Zero fighters came again on July 20, 1943. A Beaufort had just observed a Japanese naval force off Cape St George consisting of three cruisers and five destroyers—and was immediately set upon by four Zeros. The pilot made for the clouds while the turret gunner engaged the Zeros forcing one to break away. For 20 minutes, flying in and out of clouds, they dodged the Zeros. With its tanks holed, engine nacelles riddled and one tyre punctured, the Beaufort returned to a safe landing.

Attacks on Gasmata were greeted with heavy anti-aircraft fire; A9-184, 195, 210, 213 and 214, all replacement Mk VIII Beauforts, were damaged by the barrage there in late July 1943. Routine inspections, engine changes and the effects of rough airfields, were already causing high unserviceability. Now there was considerable battle damage; A9-184, for example, returned with most of its ailerons shot away.

Inevitably the occasional Beaufort went down, hit by ground fire, but on September 5, 1943 Beauforts of No 100 Squadron received a crippling blow. It was one of their many attacks on Gasmata airfield, but on that morning it was of vital importance. American and Australian transport aircraft were to drop paratroops at Nadzab and the Japanese aircraft on Gasmata had to be neutralised by cratering the runway and wrecking parked aircraft.

Ten Beauforts, led by Flt Lt R. H. Woollacott, followed an attack by Bostons. Coming in at 3 000 feet, they dived to 1 500 feet, much lower than usual, to ensure hitting aircraft dispersed along the runway. The Japanese immediately put up a box barrage through which the Beauforts passed, five of them being hit. The leader, with

Above right: Beauforts of No 100 Squadron RAAF in the Milne Bay area of New Guinea, April 1943. / *Australian War Memorial*

Right: Beaufort VIII A9-316 of No 8 Squadron with No 100 Squadron's A9-315 behind.

a badly damaged aircraft, continued on his bombing run and dropped bombs on the runway before crashing. Beaufort A9-186 crashed into the sea and another failed to return. Of those returning damaged A9-362, with a punctured tyre, ground looped on landing and was completely wrecked; fortunately the crew escaped injury.

No 100 Squadron was left at its lowest effective strength. The Commanding Officer was ill, four crews had been lost in two days, another four were grounded by the Medical Officer on completion of their operational tours and four crews, trained for general reconnaissance work, were posted to No 6 Squadron converting from Hudsons to Beauforts. This left five crews to man the 17 Beauforts on strength. Fortunately No 8 Squadron equipped with Beauforts came onto the operational scene in September 1943. Receiving Beauforts in March, they had trained in the aircraft's prime role as a torpedo-bomber, but were used immediately for attacking enemy airfields losing their first Beaufort (A9-256) on the 22nd.

Japanese fighters clashed again with a Beaufort on October 8, this time over the Solomon Sea. The six enemy aircraft approached from 3 000 feet with 1 500 feet height advantage. Flying Officer W. A. Barr turned immediately for cloud cover and jettisoned his bombs. For 37 minutes the Beaufort was chased, collecting 17 holes in its tail and empennage. By perfect pre-practised co-ordination, the aircraft was controlled by instructions from the turret gunner—except when one Zero tried to ram head-on! One Oscar was sent down smoking and a Zero out of control.

Three days later a No 6 Squadron Beaufort on patrol over St George's Channel was attacked by enemy float-planes when a convoy was spotted and attacked. A direct hit was made on a 2 000-ton coaster, and in this case the enemy aircraft were easily shaken off.

With two days' warning of an impending convoy and later intelligence on its movements, 27 Beauforts drawn from Nos 6, 8 and 100 Squadrons set out as an anti-shipping strike force at midnight on October 22, some attacking with torpedoes and others with bombs. Heavy anti-aircraft fire precluded an 'on the spot' assessment. One bomb appeared to have been dropped down a cruiser's funnel and another ship was seen on fire aft, but post-war assessments do not indicate any sinkings. A9-244 from No 8 Squadron failed to return and its fate is still not known.

Beauforts started a series of attacks on Rabaul from October 12, 1943. Reinforcements of 300 Japanese naval fighters were sent to Rabaul from November bringing Japanese air strength in the area up to its peak of 580. The Japanese put 125 aircraft into the air on November 2 to counter raiding Mitchell bombers escorted by P-38 Lightning fighters. As a result, all three Beaufort squadrons were directed to attack airfields that night and the following day. Wary this time of a box barrage, they went over at 10 000 feet. One Beaufort crew, circling over the area in the early hours trying to locate an airfield, saw the flare-path light up and a green light flash. Realising that the Japs thought him to be a friendly aircraft, the pilot took the opportunity to go in lower to drop his bombs.

Shipping strikes made by Beauforts on a convoy of Rabaul early in November were crucial for the future of the aircraft. The Beaufort was being used mainly as a close support and attack aircraft, a task now being carried out by Kittyhawk fighter-bombers which with greater speed and less bulk were less vulnerable to ground fire. An advantage of the Beaufort was its dual shipping strike and search role when the services of navigator were essential but medium bombers, such as Bostons and Mitchells, now available under Lend/Lease, would also have this facility

Above left: Typical of the narrow jungle strips from which the Australian Beauforts were forced to operate; Mk VII A9-132 depicted. / *RAAF*

Above: A9-168, an example of the thirty only Mk VAs which were, in the main, used in training units. / *RAAF*

The Beaufort was the only torpedo-bomber, but in this role it had not been successful in Pacific waters. It was now an old design, had a limited range for the vast ocean areas of the Pacific and was uncomfortable for the crews in comparison with the American bombers. Moreover, in tropical conditions in its prime role it was overloaded carrying a torpedo, which it was required to lift off from a jungle-hewn airstrip. The suggestion was made of discarding the Beaufort and disbanding the Torpedo Bombing Training Establishment at Nowra, New South Wales.

As a result of these developments the outcome of the attack off Rabaul became crucial. Aircraft were kept back from routine operations to permit a high serviceability state for the shipping strikes. The concensus of opinion in No 8 Squadron was that a formation attack was not likely to succeed because of the concentration of AA fire that could be brought to bear. It was suggested that No 6 Squadron, detailed to attack airfields to reduce aerial opposition to the torpedo-carrying aircraft, should instead bomb the shipping, causing the convoy to disperse and raising the possibility of picking off individual targets isolated from the protective fire of other ships. But No 6 Squadron pointed out that their bombs were unsuitable for shipping strikes and they were re-directed to their original targets.

In the end, only three Beauforts set out, in the early hours of the morning through heavy rain and thunderstorms. Fortunately the weather cleared as they neared Rabaul in 'V' formation, and changed to line astern at low level as they sped across Talili Bay into the harbour area. In the lead Wg Cdr G. D. Nicoll, ignoring the heavy fire from anti-aircraft guns in the harbour, aimed his aircraft towards a tanker and dropped his torpedo. His No 2 went for the cruisers escorting the convoy, and flew into a heavy barrage of AA in which his Beaufort disintegrated. Squadron Leader W. T. Quinn the No 3, weaving violently to avoid searchlights, made for the same target. After dropping his torpedo he turned back into the barrage, apparently expecting the guns would follow through in his original direction of flight. However, at night the enemy were not to know the small strength of the attack and maintained a box barrage expecting further run-ins from the same direction. In spite of this mistake, Squadron Leader Quinn and the formation leader returned to their base.

The group commander made some changes in squadron command after this attack, but was himself replaced shortly afterwards. The year ended on a sombre note for Beauforts. The Japanese struck at their jungle airfields and succeeded in damaging A9-437, one of the most recently delivered Beauforts, on December 13, and on Christmas Day A9-445, landing with wing bombs still attached, blew up killing the crew. But production was now well under way with over 500 delivered. There was no shortage of aircraft replacements, but it was the crews who counted and in the year to come the Beaufort was to be used continually and intensively on operations.

Out by Beaufort ~ Back by Boat

Beaufort A9-571 of No 100 Squadron, making a strafing run at But Mission on the Wewak coast, was hit by groundfire and the port engine was set on fire. The pilot turned the aircraft seawards to make a ditching offshore, but the cabin filled with smoke, choking the crew, forcing an immediate ditching in the shallows 20 yards from But Plantation.

Taking to the dinghy on the seaward side for cover, the crew paddled away to come under fire from the shore as soon as they left the shelter of the Beaufort. At the first burst the navigator was killed outright and the other three jumped overboard and swam, towing the dinghy seawards. Further bursts of fire killed the pilot and collapsed the dinghy, leaving only the two wireless operator/air gunners, one of whom disappeared soon afterwards.

Flying Officer R. A. Graetz, hit by a bullet which carried away the lobe of his ear and caused profuse bleeding, swam away and drifted with the current until the tide brought him ashore within 100 yards of a Jap soldier. Crawling unobserved into scrub, weak from loss of blood, he lay hidden until nightfall when the Japanese posted sentries. Moving further into the scrub he lost shirt and trousers and lay completely naked until dawn.

After dawn he searched to recover his clothes, and lay down under a bush for most of the day becoming delirious at times. Next morning, regaining his senses, he made his way towards But airfield where he saw no sign of life but a cratered runway and damaged Japanese aircraft. Finding a crater filled with clear water he spent some time bathing and drinking. Deciding to travel westward at night, he was thwarted by Japanese columns carrying lanterns and large packages. After another day without food he slept under a bush once again near the beach.

On the third day he tried building a raft of coconut logs and empty drums and tried binding it with lengths of salvaged Japanese signal wire but the raft repeatedly collapsed. Stumbling across a coastal gun emplacement, he tried to sabotage it by putting sand in the breach mechanism and down the barrel. That night he slept in a wrecked aircraft and awoke early when two Japanese soldiers carrying a machine-gun walked past.

Moving westward he came across huts that Japanese troops had recently occupied and picked up a towel and a water bottle. Passing some unattended lorries, he pulled the distributor wires out before moving on. He then found himself at the receiving end of an attack by Bostons. An escorting fighter dropped a belly tank near a tree under which he was sheltering and to add to his discomfiture it was ignited during the strafing by a tracer round. As troops appeared to be concentrating in the area he went into hiding and slept.

Next day continuing westward along a muddy track he walked straight past a Japanese soldier who continued on his way. Emboldened, he passed other troops some of whom grunted—he grunted back in acknowledgement. As

Right: Beauforts over the Milne Bay area of New Guinea, April 1943. / *Australian War Memorial*

Above: Beauforts leaving a New Guinea strip for a bombing raid with bombs carried internally, and 250lb bombs externally on wing racks. This view shows well the positioning of the landing lights in the leading edge of the wings for night landings. / *Australian War Memorial*

he was carrying the Japanese-type water-bottle, they probably thought him a fellow-countryman. The Japanese all appeared dejected, while his own spirits were rising especially having found some apple-like fruit which assuaged his hunger. For three more days he pressed on, passing close to isolated batches of troops and dodging organised parties.

While trying to cross the Danmap River, some P-39 Airacobras passed over. Two left the formation to circle round him when he waved a small parachute he had picked up from a parafrag bomb earlier, to use as a sleeping bag. Expecting a Catalina to follow up and rescue him he lay in wait on the bank. But it was an American PT boat that arrived and he was too weak to swim out to it.

Firing broke out from the shore, and while the guns of the PT boat replied the crew shot lines ashore, but Graetz was now even too weak to hold on. Eventually two PT crew members swam ashore with a small raft and ferried the airman to their boat and safety.

From Strike to Support. Australasia 1944

In January 1944 Beauforts were supporting Australian troops in New Britain and New Ireland. On the 17th, with Spitfire and Kittyhawk escorts, 32 attacked an enemy camp on the Amgen River losing A9-387 of No 6 Squadron through engine trouble. The crew were rescued by a Catalina flying boat. Similarly, on May 22 when A9-468 was hit by anti-aircraft fire off Wewak and forced to ditch, a Catalina landed and took off the crew.

More Beaufort strikes were made on the Wewak area than on any other territory. It was here that 40 000 Japanese under Lieutenant-General Adachi held desperately on to a tract of land in New Guinea, relatively close to Australia and a menace to further Allied conquests along the island stepping stones to Imperial Japan.

The Beaufort was committed now to the support role and was being trimmed for this task. A different turret, built in a new factory at Fairfield, Victoria, was being fitted in the 561st and subsequent Beauforts coming off production early in the year. This was the Mk VE turret taking 5-inch calibre machine guns. While the need for defensive armament was receding, the guns were being used more than ever for ground strafing. However, not until over a year later was sufficient stocks of .5 ammunition available for general use.

A new version made its first flight on February 4. This was A9-201 allotted to the Department of Aircraft Production for liaison work and progress chasing between the various factories producing parts and the two assembly lines at Mascot and Fisherman's Bend. First it was stripped of armament fittings, armour plate, bomb racks and other operational equipment, saving 2 000lb on the all-up weight. Without the turret a new smooth dorsal line was possible, and without the internal operational equipment seats for five passengers were fitted in addition to the crew of three. In this configuration the Beaufort reached a speed of 300mph, and could carry up to a 4 000lb pay load at 284mph. A welded tube pannier, with quick release pins, could carry up to 600lb slung from the bomb bay. After tests, the bomb bay was enlarged to enclose the pannier and reduce drag, but it was not considered practical as there was insufficient ground clearance for airstrip work and it was re-converted to its earlier transport form.

At this time part of the Japanese Combined Fleet visited Singapore and there was some apprehension that it might strike westward to Ceylon—to where RAF Beauforts had been sent—or eastwards to Australia. Defences in the North-West Area were increased, including Nos 1 & 2 Squadrons which had discarded Hudsons for Beauforts. In addition to passive patrols, strikes were also carried out across the Timor Sea to attack Japanese bases, particularly at Koepang, in the former Netherland East

Above: Viewed from a participating aircraft, Beauforts set out for a daylight attack on Rabaul, January 17, 1944. / *Australian War Memorial*

Below and right: The Beaufort IX transport version with re-designed mid-fuselage and armour and armament removed. / *Bristol Aeroplane Company*

Indies. Here, too, there was the hazard of anti-aircraft fire and No 1 Squadron lost both A9-509 and 541 in an attack on Japanese barracks at Penfui, Timor, on May 8.

The veteran Beaufort squadrons, Nos 8 and 100, moved into Aitape in June 1944 following Allied landings on New Guinea's northern coast about a hundred miles from the port of Wewak. They were in time to play their part in meeting the Japanese counter-attack, one of the two squadrons mounting 56 strikes in one day to repulse the advancing enemy. Their major contribution was in frustrating the Japanese efforts in getting Wewak airstrip operating, so that the Australian troops enjoyed the benefits of almost complete air superiority.

With a landing in New Britain pending, the work of the two squadrons was divided as they were required to supplement No 6 Squadron's bombing attacks on Rabaul, as part of the softening up process. However, reinforcement soon came with No 7 Squadron moving up from Northern Australia into Aitape to form a Beaufort Wing under Wing Commander Eric Cooper, AFC.

Here the Beaufort was being used in a close support role, attacking targets requested by the army. The Japanese had long since stopped reinforcing by merchant ships, so that the Beauforts were no longer required to operate in their designed role. Supplies came surreptitiously by submarine at night or by barges hugging the coast by day and crossing the open sea at night. It fell to the Beauforts to destroy the supplies after they had landed, by raiding dumps and razing every native hut in the Japanese troop areas.

To reduce traffic further, US Navy PT boats were called in; Beauforts co-operated by dropping flares to illuminate targets for the PTs. In four nights they were instrumental in the destruction of 13 barges and damage to 13 others by the PT boats, as well as their direct contribution of two direct hits with 500lb bombs on barges.

Part of support role entailed plastering defensive ridges, where the Japanese troops were entrenched using the roots of forest trees as part of their emplacements. These trees had to be uprooted by high explosive bombs as artillery shells would often plough into the ridges without exploding. The army would mark the targets with mortar shells, as soon as they heard the Beauforts coming in to attack.

In its close support role, supply dropping became a prime requirement and special containers to fit into the bomb-bay, known as 'storpedoes', were built. As these were often in short supply, Warrant Officer Jack Ceasar designed a wooden crate that could be made locally with automatic opening doors.

One of the most successful air-drops by Beauforts was that of barbed wire. The Australian troops had wind of an impending attack accompanied by the usual frenzied *banzai* charge. Wire was immediately requested and dropped, enabling the troops to wire round their own positions. When the charge came, the Japs were frustrated by the wire and picked off by riflemen as they tried to disentangle themselves.

In these support roles, there was a need for a transport Beaufort at the front. Work was put in hand at the Repair and Modification Centre at Essendon, Victoria, to modify 46 Beauforts in store to transport versions, similar to A9-201 mentioned earlier. In service these were designated the Mk IX. Production had finally stopped in August 1944, when the plants went over to Beaufighters. The final total production of Beauforts in Australia was as follows:

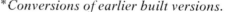

Serial Nos of 700 built	Mk	Pratt & Whitney R-1830	Propeller
A9-1 to 50	V	S3C4-G	Curtiss electric
A9-51 to 90	VI	S1C3-G	Curtiss electric
A9-91 to 150	VII	S1C3-G	Hamilton standard
A9-151 to 180	VA	S3C4-G	Hamilton standard
A9-181 to 700	VIII	S3C4-G	Curtiss electric
A9-701 to 746*	IX	S3C4-G	Curtiss electric

Conversions of earlier built versions.

Above: Servicing Beaufort VIII A9-255 in New Guinea, April 25, 1944 under a double screen—a camouflage net to hide the aircraft from the Japanese and a canvas to shield the ground crew from the sun and, at this moment, the bowser crew. / *RAAF*

Left: Beaufort VIIIs of No 6 Squadron RAAF assemble for take-off on a bombing raid. It will be seen that the remote-controlled rearward-firing chin guns have been replaced by forward-firing hand-held twin guns in the nose for strafing. / *RAAF*

Centre right: The last Beaufort built, delivered August 31, 1944, shown here with a 'Bugs Bunny' insignia on nose. ASV 'yagi' aerials can be seen under each wing. / *CAC*

Bottom right: Beaufort of No 8 Squadron, RAAF, over the Wewak area of New Guinea, 1944.

The Maximum Effort. Australasia 1945

In the last year of the war Beauforts continued to hammer at the enemy. To take just one day's activity—January 23, 1945, No 7 Squadron sent out eight Beauforts to bomb Balif Village where Japanese troops were encamped. Seven or eight huts were destroyed, others damaged and 2 150 rounds from their guns ripped around the area and through most of the huts in the village. No 8 Squadron had two Beauforts out on normal daily search pattern. No 100 Squadron dropped six tons of bombs, including fragmentation and incendiaries, on another village—Aluma where a large fire was started.

Huts, enemy foxholes, outrigger canoes, all featured in the targets strafed. There were also occasional sea searches, leaflet raids and photo reconnaissance trips, but in main activity was bombing and strafing. Japanese shortages due to the Beauforts' operations led to diminishing opposition from anti-aircraft fire; but since both on March 13 and 16 No 100 Squadron had a Beaufort blow up in the air when over enemy foxholes, it would appear that the Japanese were becoming marksmen with small arms. Certainly the Beauforts went in low at times. One No 100 Squadron aircraft dropped 15 30lb incendiaries on huts at Mainga from a mere 50 feet.

Although still classed as GR/B (General Reconnaissance/Bomber) squadrons, the Beaufort squadrons were now practically restricted to bombing and strafing. Nos 7, 8 and 100 Squadrons continued harassing attacks in the Wewak area while No 6 divided attention between the Cape Orford area and supporting attacks in the Wewak area, before being switched to attacks on the much-bombed Rabaul. Then No 15 Squadron came on the scene to add to those hammering the Wewak area.

To give an idea of the intensity of Beaufort operations the RAAF Command Summary for one day in the period is given, showing the preponderance of work carried out by the Beaufort Squadrons:—

RAAF Command Summary March 30, 1945

Rabaul Area

4 Beauforts of No 6 Squadron. Enemy concentrations at Lamingi (12 miles NW of Adler Bay) attacked with three tons; huts demolished and damaged, 10 600 × .303 expended.

12 B-24s. Attacked aeroplane parks at Vunakanau and Tobera bombed with 48 tons; results unobserved.

Open Bay Area

6 Beauforts of No 6 Squadron. Huts and troops at Matalaili River bombed and strafed with three tons and 8 700 × .303; no results observed.

Wewak Area

4 Beauforts of No 15 Squadron. Grumbangi (2½ miles NW of Ambunti), Seseriman, Ambanti and village, 3½ miles NW of Ambunti, bombed and strafed with two tons and 10 600 × .303.

4 Beauforts of No 15 Squadron. Seseriman Village bombed and strafed and several huts destroyed; two tons and 10 560 × .303 expended.

1 Beaufort of No 100 Squadron. Five huts at Ulupu village opportunity and bombed huts in vicinity of Cape Wom. ¼ ton dropped and 2 100 × .303 fired.

1 Beaufort of No 7 Squadron. Village, four miles S.S.E. of Maprik, and two good huts, 5½ miles SSE of Maprik, strafed with 1 900 × .303.

6 Beauforts of No 100 Squadron. Enemy positions, approx five miles NE of Maprik, bombed and strafed, with good coverage. Approx. 2½ tons dropped and 4 000 × .303 fired.

1 Beaufort of No 100 Squadron. Five huts at Ulupu village (three miles SW of Yamil) destroyed; four huts also destroyed and others left burning at Bukinara; 16 × 30lb incendiaries dropped.

9 Beauforts of No 8 Squadron. Ridge, six miles east of But, occupied by enemy, bombed, with excellent results; 4½ tons bombs dropped.

4 Beauforts of No 7 Squadron. Enemy position, three miles NW of Maprik, bombed with 2¾ tons and strafed with 8 500 × .303.

5 Beauforts of No 100 Squadron. Village, four miles N of Maprik, bombed and incendiaries fell among huts south of the village, destroying eight; approx 4½ tons dropped and 5 550 × .303 fired.

5 A-20s (Bostons) and 6 B-25s (Mitchells). Kulaura, Ulupu and Yoibi River villages bombed and strafed; one bomb fell amongst six huts and five huts were fired by strafing in the Kalauri-Ulupu area; numerous huts and buildings at Yoibi village hit causing fires and an explosion; six tons, 11 725 × .5 expended.

The scale of attacks intensified and in one week of April Beauforts expended 118 550 rounds and 55 tons of bombs. This was part of a softening up process for a landing along the Wewak littoral, eleven miles to the East, to further contain the Japanese. Under the cover of guns from HMS *Newfoundland* and HMAS *Hobart*, and Beauforts circling overhead, the assault troops soon landed, consolidated and expanded their beachhead. To maintain ship-to-shore communication and an overall control, a Beaufort was fitted out as a flying wireless station. Major J. Leitch, an Air-Army Liaison Officer, flying in this aircraft, kept touch with both the troops ashore commanded by Major-General Stevens and the flagship off-shore, relaying messages as necessary.

From June 1945 .50 ammunition became available in quantity for the Beauforts strafing work. Up to the end of

Above right: A No 7 Squadron RAAF Beaufort drops supplies to Australian troops in the Aitape district of New Guinea. / *Australian War Memorial*

Right: Scene at Aitape, New Guinea. In the foreground is Beaufort VIII A9-486 'Scotty's Homin Pidgin', flown by Flying Officer Chris Scott, which made 139 strikes against the Japanese, hence the rows of bomb symbols chalked up beneath the cockpit side-window. / *Australian War Memorial*

Above: A truly symbolic picture of the Australian-built Beaufort as A9-700, the last Beaufort built, flies over Sydney Harbour. In this picture the folding direction finding loop can be seen fully extended on the cabin top. / *Bristol Aeroplane Company*

Left: Return to Singapore. The first Beaufort to fly to Singapore in October 1945 shortly after re-occupation by Allied troops. / *IWM*

Below: In a similar way to RAF crews in Bomber Command, some RAAF Beaufort crews marked bombing missions on their aircraft. Since the extent of the markings are not apparent in the photograph shown of this aircraft on page 75 they are amplified here.

June Beauforts had made 8 000 sorties, dropped 8 000 000lb of bombs and expended a million rounds of ammunition.

In the very last month of the war in British New Guinea came the most intense, concentrated and sustained efforts by Beaufort aircraft in the whole of the war. This was again in the notorious Wewak area of mountainous tiger-infested country. At times over 30 Beauforts were in the air together.

The attacks continued for a fortnight and that on the 15th was the last Beaufort attack of the war. According to the official report on that day '30 Beauforts of Nos 7, 8 & 100 Squadrons strafed unspecified targets in the Muschu Island area and dropped bombs on enemy positions in the vicinity of Kiarivu (Wewak). Majority of bombs fell on the target areas; otherwise in the vicinity; 25¼ tons of bombs dropped, 19 700 × .303 rounds expended'. That same day, over the Bougainville area, three Beauforts flew over enemy positions at minimum altitude dropping leaflets informing Japanese troops of their Emperor's acceptance of peace terms. On August 18 a message to all formations from Allied Command, read: 'Until further orders there will be no flights over Japanese held land territory'.

By the end of the war transport versions of the Beaufort were serving in communications units and local air supply units, playing a part in the withdrawal from the tropical areas, back to the mainland. There was no further military tasks for the Beauforts and the type was not granted a Civil Certificate of Airworthiness. The flying days of the Australian Beauforts were almost over. A plague of grasshoppers in 1946 did lead to some being used with spraying rigs, but apart from a few kept in store as an emergency reserve for some years, the Beaufort was scrapped. No-one in the late 40's or early 50's thought of preserving anything so common as a Beaufort; in consequence, not one has survived intact.

Strangely it is in America that an Australian-built Beaufort has a chance of preservation. At 'Warbirds Aviation Museum', Mildura Airport, California, there is the fuselage and wing centre-section of Beaufort VII A9-143. Also in California, at 'Yesterday's Air', Chino Airport, David Tallachet has plans for Mk VIIIs A9-577 and 679, plus another unidentified, to be shipped to America from locations in New Guinea, to provide parts for one complete Beaufort. So there are hopes that at least one full specimen of a Beaufort may be preserved. Has anyone a spare Mk XII torpedo? Essential that warhead be removed!

Beaufort Squadron Code Letters of Royal Australian Air Force

No 1	NA	No 13	SF
No 2	KO	No 14	PN
No 6	FX	No 15	DD
No 7	KT	No 32	JM
No 8	UV	No 100	QH

Appendices

BEAUFORT PRODUCTION BREAKDOWN
1938-1944

British-built 1938-43

Mk	Quantity
I	1 013
II	167
TII	249
III	(0) project
IV	(1) conversion

Total 1 429 built
(less 3 actually delivered
due to crashes on test)

Australian-built 1941-44

Mk	Quantity
V	50
VA	30
VI	40
VII	60
VIII	520
IX	(46) conversions

Total 700 built

Royal Air Force Beaufort Serial Allocations
L4441-4518, L9790-9838, L9851-9897, L9932-9972, N1000-1047, N1074-1109 Mk I. N1110 Mk II prototype. N1111-1118, N1145-1186, W6467-6506, W6518-6543, X8916-8939, AW187-221, AW234-243 Mk I. AW244-253, AW271-315, AW335-384, DD870-911, DD927-944 Mk II. DD945-959, DD974-999, DE108-126, DW802-836, DW851-898, DW913-962, DW977-999, DX114-157, EK969-999, EL123-141, JM431-470, JM496-517, JM545-593, LR885-908, LR920-963, LR976-999, LS113-128 Mk I. LS129 Mk II. LS130-149, ML430-476, ML489-524, ML540-586, ML599-635, ML649-692, ML705-722 Mk II(T). Additionally T9540-9569, T9583-9618, T9624-9657 was allotted for Mk IIs to have been built in Australia of which seven were completed and renumbered in A9 Australian series below.

Royal Australian Air Force Beaufort Serial Allocations.
A9-prefix common to all. 1-50 Mk V, 51-90 Mk VI, 91-150 Mk VII, 151-180 Mk VA, 181-700 Mk VIII (46 of these converted to Mk IX and re-numbered 701-746).

BEAUFORT DIVERSIONS FROM RAF

Royal Australian Air Force: L4448 (1).

Royal Canadian Air Force: L9967, L9968, N1005, N1006, N1007, N1021, N1026, N1027, N1029, N1030, N1045, N1078, N1107, W6473, W6484. (15).

South African Air Force: L9940, L9941, L9954, L9956, L9957, L9960, N1004, N1008, N1046, N1047, N1076, N1145, DD883, DW886, DW892, DW896, DW898, DW946. (18)

Turkish Air Force: DW893, DW930, DW945, DW954, DW960, DW981, DW985, DX125, DX144, DX147, DX149, DX153, ML492, ML495, ML499, ML500, ML501, ML506, ML515, ML518, ML542, ML543, ML544, ML545. (24)

BEAUFORT DATA

Construction
The fuselage was of monocoque construction with duralumin formers and hiduminium stringers, covered with Alclad sheet flush-riveted into position. Alclad was a light alloy sandwiched between an aluminium coating of high purity, which combined light weight, with strength and a high resistance to corrosion. Wings were similarly of dural and hiduminium, covered with Alclad. An exception was the main control surfaces, rudder, ailerons and elevators, which were covered in doped fabric. The whole could be broken down into three major components of wings, forward fuselage and rear fuselage so that in dispersal production as planned in Australia, any major portion would match up to any other.

Dimensions
Wingspan: 57ft 10in	Length overall: 44ft 3in
Height: 12ft 5in	Wing Area: 503sq ft
Track: 18ft 0in	

Weights
Tare: 13 107lb Mk I, 14 074lb Mk II, 14 070lb Mk VIII
Loaded with torpedo: 21 228lb Mk I, 22 083lb Mk II

Tankage
Fuel capacity: 570 gallons (DTD230/87 octane)
Oil capacity: 39 gallons (DTD109)

Performance
Maximum speed (Mk I without torpedo): 271.5mph at 6 500 feet
Maximum speed (Mk I with Mk XII torpedo): 263mph at 6 500 feet
Maximum speed (Mk II with Mk XII torpedo): 270mph at 14 500 feet
Maximum cruising speed (Mk I without torpedo): 255mph at 6 500 feet
Maximum cruising speed (with Mk XII torpedo): 225mph Mk I & 230mph Mk II at 6 500 feet
Take-off run (Mk I without torpedo): 255 yards
Take-off run (Mk I with Mk XII torpedo): 295 yards
Service ceiling: 16 500 feet Mk I, 18 000 feet Mks II/VIII
Normal range: 1 600 miles Mk I, 1 450 miles Mk II
Endurance (all Mks): Approx 6 hours
Initial rate of climb: 1 200 feet per minute

Armament
Maximum of 2 000lb bombs or Mk XII or Mk XIV torpedo and up to 9 × .303 machine-guns, with some substitution of .5 machine-guns in Australian-built models in 1945. Load variations and gun position variation as given in text and captioning.

Beaufort Marks

Mk	Engines—2 Per aircraft	Remarks
I	Bristol Taurus II, III, VI, XII or XVI	Main production version
II	Pratt & Whitney Twin Wasp R1830-S3C4-G	Late production version
III	Rolls-Royce Merlin XX	Project only
IV	Bristol Taurus XX	Experiment, AW372 only
V	Pratt & Whitney Twin Wasp R-1830-S3C4-G	Curtiss propellers
VA	Pratt & Whitney Twin Wasp R1830-S3C4-G	Hamilton propellers
VI	Pratt & Whitney Twin Wasp R1830-S1C3-G	Curtiss propellers
VII	Pratt & Whitney Twin Wasp R1830-S1C3-G	Hamilton propellers
VIII	Pratt & Whitney Twin Wasp R1830-S3C4-G	Curtiss propellers
IX	Pratt & Whitney Twin Wasp R1830-S3C4-G	Transport conversion of Mk VIII

Notes: The original Mk I Taurus was not used on the Beaufort. The prototype L4441 was fitted with the Mk III and the majority of early production the Mk II. Modified Mk II engines to Mk III standard were designated initially Mk IIA and later re-designated Mk VI. These early marks were rated at 860/900hp at 2 800rpm, with a maximum power of 1 065hp at 3 225rpm. The improved Mk XII and XVI had a maximum of 1 130hp. Standard propeller with Taurus engines was the de Havilland Type DH5/19 constant speed airscrew.

The Twin Wasp, giving 1 200hp, was fitted with either Curtiss-electric or Hamilton bracket type variable pitch airscrews as tabled.

It has been ascertained since first publication that Beauforts N1010, N1031, N1032 and N1111 were also diverted to the South African Air Force and EK976 to the Turkish Air Force.

Left and below: Alpha and Omega represented by L4441 and A9-700 the very first, and the very last, Beaufort built. / *Real Photographs and RAAF*

Above: The first Australian-built Beaufort bearing its original RAF serial. This aircraft was retrospectively included in the A9 Royal Australian Air Force serial series.

Below: Beauforts in the background at Fishermen's Bend where attention is being paid to a British-built Beaufighter, a type that was soon to replace Beauforts on the lines at this factory.